Barbra Streisand

Barbra Streisand

A Biography

Peter Carrick

ROBERT HALE · LONDON

ISBN 0 7090 4432 1

Robert Hale Limited
Clerkenwell House
Clerkenwell Green
London EC1R 0HT

Photoset in Palatino in North Wales by
Derek Doyle & Associates, Mold, Clwyd.
Printed in Great Britain by
St Edmundsbury Press, Bury St Edmunds, Suffolk.
Bound by Hunter & Foulis.

Contents

To David Boyce, mentor and friend, for his tutelage, guidance and example in the early years and his continued inspiration since.

Illustrations

PICTURE CREDITS

Lynn Pounder: 1–6, 8–9, 12–13, 17–23. CBS: 2–3. CBS Fox Video: 5. Ellbar Productions: 4, 22. Columbia: 6, 8–11, 13–15, 23. Paramount UIP: 7. British Film Institute: 7, 10–11, 14–15. Universal UIP: 12. Alpha Photographic (Photo: David Parker): 16. MGM: 18–20.

1 *No Oscar for* Yentl

There was near hysteria among Barbra Streisand fans when her film *Yentl* failed to make the Oscar listings in 1983. The snub was to be condemned by an increasing number of movie buffs at best as a devastating example of Hollywood injustice. At worst it was branded the most blatantly cynical manifestation of an awards system which, while masquerading beneath a veneer of objectivity and lofty ideals and despite its massive international media focus, all too often seemed exposed to accusations of injustice, prejudice and self-interest.

The problem is two-fold. Since there is no unchallengeable yardstick by which a film or an actor's or actress's performance can be judged, votes are cast on the basis of a number of subjective personal assessments; and, secondly, because so much money and professional glorification is riding on the announcement of the winners, or even the nominations, the system has scant defence against allegations of ill-meaning pressure, arrogance, collusion, soliciting and impropriety. Within this framework it was perhaps too much to contemplate that a film which was so much out of the ordinary, and at the same time such a strong Streisand vehicle, ever stood much chance of an award. The fact that it received a number of nominations in the minor categories, with nothing more than a commendable performance from Amy Irving for best support-ing actress perhaps being the best of the bunch, only served to compound the injustice. Salvation of sorts came in the form of the top award to Michel Legrand and Alan and Marilyn Bergman in the Music (Original Score) category, so justly deserved. But for Streisand, who conceived the idea of putting

9

Yentl on screen and who ultimately became the first woman in cinema history to direct, produce, write and star in a title role, there was nothing. Not even an acknowledgement for effort or endeavour.

But then, Barbra Streisand, supremely talented and accepted even by many of her critics as the greatest female entertainer in the world, is not renowned for being likeable. Nor is she much loved as an entertainer, even though she is widely admired and warmly acclaimed for her rich qualities as a singer, actress and comedienne.

Her obsessional approach to her art form is not only seen to be potentially disruptive to anyone who needs to direct or discipline her, but costs her dearly in personal relationships. From the time she read *Yentl, the Yeshiva Boy* in 1968, when she was twenty-six, to make the film and then later, to star in it, became a crusading passion. Tenaciously she set about turning the vision into reality, first buying the sole rights to the story in 1972 and then hawking it around for financial backing. One studio after another thumbed it down. They were turned off by its uncompromising ethnic story line about a young early twentieth-century Eastern European Jewish girl with a passion to study learned books, an opportunity denied her as to all females of her faith at that time because of the Jewish culture. Herself proudly Jewish, and still perhaps inwardly lamenting the loss of a father who died before she was old enough to know him, Streisand found herself drawn to the story about the young girl who dared to ask 'why?' and who, filled with the joy of learning, finds herself with no choice after her father dies but to disguise herself as a young man so that, in the words of the soundtrack, she can pursue all her 'sweet imagined possibilities' which the world has to offer.

But the studios found the combination of Streisand's uncompromising and 'difficult' personality and her insistence on taking over so much control of the picture, simply too risky. A mid-1970s off-Broadway production of the story which achieved moderate success neither helped nor hindered the prospects for Barbra's venture. Some five years later Orion Pictures, after announcing in 1979 that they would go ahead with the production of the film and back it to the extent of $12 to $15 million, decided to pull out. The reason was a later budget assessment of $17 million combined with nagging doubts about

Barbra's all-round capacity to deliver after she had declared her firm intention to produce as well as direct the picture.

By this time, early in 1981, Streisand had already worked tirelessly on the movie, not only in an effort to make it happen, but on the crucial early detail of script, locations, production and musical score. In midsummer 1980, several months or so before Orion came forward with their ill-fated decision to cancel, composer Michel Legrand and lyricists Marilyn and Alan Bergman had been recruited to the project by Barbra. Lyrics were soon underway and the score was being finished off when Orion aborted the venture.

Chances now that *Yentl* would ever see the light of day appeared remote, if they existed at all. Hollywood was fleetingly becalmed, cash-starved in the face of falling profits. Dead-cert ideas were what mattered for the moment. Any fringe venture which had Streisand, less than eighteen months away from her fortieth birthday, dressing up as a young man and even going through a form of marriage, stood little chance of being taken seriously. But Barbra was grimly determined that her picture would be made.

Both Paramount and Warner Brothers were reportedly interested in doing a deal, but nothing materialized. Streisand could not accept the loss of creative control implicit in any deal with Paramount. Not for some months after Orion's withdrawal did Streisand's burning ambition seem to have any real possibility of being realized. Then United Artists, curiously a studio which had not yet made a Streisand movie, swallowed hard, took a deep breath and agreed to go ahead and underwrite the picture, fixing an inflexible budget at a not inconsiderable $14.5 million. The studio had been ambitious for some time to release a Barbra Streisand movie and, while the United Artists moguls might well have cursed their ill-luck in being unable to divert Barbra from her obsession, they wanted her badly enough to take her, *Yentl* package and all.

Barbra's agreement with United Artists, soon to be merged with MGM, was formally announced on Monday, 22 June 1981. She was ecstatic. For thirteen years, since she had taken Hollywood by storm in her first movie *Funny Girl* in 1968, she had lived with the vision of *Yentl*, though the movie was still as yet unnamed. The project had dominated her professional and private life. Her commitment to her ambition had already been prodigious and now, to secure the deal, she was willing to accept, by normal standards, punitive contractual obligations imposed by the studio. In safeguarding their own interests United Artists leaned heavily on Streisand's cult-like devotion to her project. They pushed her into making concessions and giving guarantees knowing how much the venture meant to her. Having already put $500,000 of her own money into the project, she now gave assurances on budgeting and scheduling, against financial penalties and, above all, against the risk of losing the creative control of the picture which she had always insisted she must have.

In addition, she agreed to cash terms grossly disproportionate to the enormous executive and creative responsibilities required of her to see the film through. She claimed, for instance, that she did not get paid for the work she had done and organized on the script, and she was to receive only a token fee for directing. But for Barbra the project was all-important. The vision looked set to become reality as she proclaimed to the world: 'Nothing mattered to me except getting this movie made.'

But a further hitch developed as management changes and studio battles among United Artists' hierarchy held up the start date, at first scheduled for September 1981. It was well into 1982 before she was given the green light to begin the monumental task of casting the picture, completing a part-finished script, and researching in elaborate detail the numerous segments of a sensitive story to ensure its visual authenticity. For her to work a nineteen-to-twenty-hour day was not uncommon. Her schedule was overwhelming, the worries and anxieties at times hardly bearable.

Take the crucial business of casting. To see names like 1990s superstars Richard Gere and Michael Douglas both turn down the key role of Avigdor, Yentl's attractive fellow-student with whom she finds herself falling in love, must have been demoralizing. Her hand-picked cast was finally bereft of major box-office names from the film world, Avigdor being played by Broadway *Evita* stage star and film discovery Mandy Patinkin, whose role as the immigrant Jewish artist Tateh in the film *Ragtime* was, as *The Movie* observed, 'pure joy'.

For the role of Hadass, Avigdor's charmingly wide-eyed innocent fiancée, Barbra looked first to Carol Kane, who had starred in the Jewish immigrant story *Hester Street* in 1975. But this idea was abandoned in favour of a younger actress, Barbra's attention then focusing on Amy Irving. But Irving wasn't really interested and was won over only after Streisand patiently spent time with her explaining the depth of the role in detail and the delicacy and sensitivity of the picture. Irving said later that Barbra's consuming dedication to the project impressed her greatly, and influenced her in making up her mind to take the part.

Extensive personal reconnaissance in Eastern Europe preceded the selection of Czechoslovakia as the country most authentically representative of the landscape of early Poland during the period in which the film is set. The script, which would go through eight separate rewrites in ten years and in the end was to absorb nine haunting, highly emotional melodies to become an impressive musical presentation through the vision of lyricists Marilyn and Alan Bergman (who first planted the idea of turning it into 'a film with music' seriously in Barbra's mind when she was looking at the story in purely dramatic terms), faltered in the face of a strike called by the Writers' Guild of America. But later it was the experienced and highly regarded British playwright and screen writer Jack Rosenthal to whom Barbra turned to give her what she wanted from a script which was crucial to the core of the story and matched her own feelings regarding the finer points of appreciation, understanding and sensitivity. Jack, perhaps best known for his highly acclaimed award-winning play *Bar Mitzvah Boy* in 1976, now became her last and certainly most important collaborator on the *Yentl* script. He worked for eight months at Barbra's London hotel and at his London home, and was to share the final credit, along with Barbra, for scripting *Yentl*.

Barbra, who in the very early days stood out strongly against appearing in the picture at all, preferring to concentrate on directing, and because she considered the part called for a younger girl, for commercial reasons had long since accepted the title role of *Yentl*. The main casting was completed when Nehemiah Persoff agreed to play Papa. Even this announcement concealed yet another example of how the project seemed consistently bedevilled, for Persoff was a second choice, the casting being confirmed after first choice Morris Carnovsky died unexpectedly following a heart attack. But what a wonderfully sensitive performance Persoff was to give.

Production work on *Yentl* ended in October 1982 and for almost another year Barbra divided her time between America and the UK sorting out production detail. Its world première in November 1983 was at Hollywood's Cinerama Dome and created such attention that a second screening was necessary, run concurrently in New York. Later that month it was shown in a selected number of venues in the United States through an exclusive prior-showing arrangement and went out on general release in that country just before Christmas. Its European release won the top accolade of a Royal première held in London in spring 1984.

After more than fifteen long, wearisome years – surely one of the longest gestation periods in motion-picture history, Barbra's pilgrimage was at an end. As she visited several countries, making exhausting tours promoting the picture, she was able to take deep and lasting pleasure from the enthusiastic acclamation of *Yentl* by many critics and was overjoyed when picture-goers everywhere, and particularly in Britain and Continental Europe, got in line to give this first Barbra Streisand film in four years, and her first musical film in seven, the warmest and most rapturous of welcomes.

In box-office terms, and for a film outside the 'popular' mode, it turned out to be a winner, reaching number three in its season of release behind the blockbusters *Terms of Endearment* and *Sudden Impact*. Within four years *Yentl* had grossed more than four times its original cost and there were to be plenty of critical honours for the venture. Even if the Academy of Motion Picture Arts and Sciences chose to ignore her creative and inspirational one-woman effort in their annual Oscar awards, she did enjoy the not inconsiderable consolation of seeing the picture receive six Hollywood Golden Globe nominations, winning two awards, one for best musical picture, the other in the best director category; and her soundtrack album of the picture became a triple platinum seller.

Barbra's official reaction to the Oscar lockout was surprisingly relaxed. She said it was maybe that they just didn't like the picture. What appeared to hurt her more perhaps was the reaction of the author of the book on which the screenplay had been based. Isaac Bashevis Singer, who had written an early version of the film script, had never been happy about the interpretation Streisand anticipated for his basic short story, reputedly written by him in about half a day. Despite his antagonism, Barbra invited him to the New York première, but he declined ungratiously. Dismissing the obvious extension of scale and vision necessary to transform his slim twenty-page story into a full-length feature film, Singer complained at the way Streisand had distorted and changed his basic theme. Afterwards he protested testily at what he felt to be an over-projection of Streisand at the expense of Yentl. But many considered Singer's attitude was because he had grossly underestimated the value of his story when he sold the rights and that, as a result, Barbra was able to pick it up at a giveaway price when compared with the massive costs of filming.

Despite her surprisingly restrained and controlled public responses, Barbra none the less was angry and bitterly disappointed at not receiving an Oscar for *Yentl*. She honestly felt that she had earned the award and was hurt that what she and countless others both inside and outside the business at that time saw as her greatest work, was brutally ignored. But while the Academy of Motion Picture Arts and Sciences, for whatever reason and in the opinion of many in Hollywood and elsewhere, chose to insult the outstanding and individual talent of Barbra Streisand, she would ultimately gain from this high-level charade. For in their obsessive dislike of Streisand, they not only devalued the Oscars in the eyes of many, but did enormous good for the prestige and reputation of Barbra. For herself, she said later that her true reward for *Yentl* was in the process itself of making the picture; in being given the opportunity of transforming her dream into reality. She gained a new esteem and a professional dimension in a world which meant so much to her, a world in which she had chosen to express her talents, the world of movie making which had first filled her mind and consumed her desires as a skinny schoolgirl in Brooklyn almost thirty years before.

2 A Star Grows in Brooklyn

The world was at war in April 1942. The United States had been hauled into the conflict four months earlier when the Japanese attacked the US Pacific Fleet in Pearl Harbor on Sunday, 7 December 1941. In April the Japanese captured the Bataan peninsular in the Philippines, taking 36,000 prisoners, and in an act of psychological bravado, American B-25s responded with a lightening raid on Tokyo and other Japanese cities, though little damage was done.

These were stirring times and the birth of a healthy daughter to Diana and Emanuel Streisand on Friday, 24 April 1942, at their comfortable middle-class apartment home on Pulaski Street in Brooklyn, New York, attracted no more than the usual passing interest in the neighbourhood. But for Diana (née Rosen) and Emanuel the arrival of their daughter was welcomed with love and affection, a baby sister for their six-year-old son Sheldon to complete a devoted family. They named her Barbara Joan.

No one could have foreseen the baby's glistening future as a professional entertainer of international stature some twenty years or so hence. For, although her mother had fleetingly wondered about becoming a singer before her marriage, because she had a nice voice and had even cut an experimental record, there was no real hint of a show-biz dynasty either on her mother's or father's side of the family. Emanuel was an academic of some potential and after working hard and gaining a creditable PhD in education, was building a successful career taking classes in English and psychology. Diana was the daughter of a skilled garment cutter, who was also a cantor at

17

the local synagogue. Both Jewish and committed to their faith, they had married in 1935 after dating for about three years.

At the time of Barbara Joan's birth popular music was dominated by the big, swinging bands of Glenn Miller, Count Basie, Woody Herman, Stan Kenton and other legendary leaders, while Hollywood was at the height of its power and influence, an untouchable 'Shangri-la' where dreams could come true for an hour or so for the price of a cinema seat. Whole nations were picture-house junkies and a growing Barbara Joan was to be no different. It didn't matter to her that she was not the prettiest of children, nor that in her early teens she would be already developing a profile different from the classical perfection demanded by Hollywood, for by then she had decided to become someone special. Though who could have imagined that by the time she had reached her mid-twenties she would be one of Hollywood's hottest properties and one of the world's greatest stars?

But that factual projection was a world away from the dark, uncertain days on Pulaski Street following her birth. Barbara Joan's parents shared the privations of a generation shattered first by the effects of the stock-market crash in the early 1930s and then the onset of a world-war catastrophy. Yet they were better off than many of their contemporaries. Emanuel accepted the importance of personal learning in the process of building a good and prosperous future for himself and his family. He had a good job with prospects to look forward to and already had managed to provide for his wife and young children a good standard of living in a comfortable home in a district of Brooklyn which, if years later was to degenerate into the notoriety of an inner-city slum, was at that time quite a reasonable place in which to live. There were parks, local shops and neighbourhood cinemas in what was then a predominantly middle-class, white community. Flatbush and Williamsburg, where Barbara grew up, consisted largely of middle-income Jewish families, many living in the several-storey brick apartment buildings which were features of the area.

Most of all the Streisands were blissfully happy. Until there came in the summer of 1943 that devastating blow which was to change the course of baby Barbara's life. Emanuel had gone to summer camp and while there tragically suffered a cerebral haemorrhage and died, though it has been reported that only recently Barbra learned that he had died from a poorly treated epileptic fit following a head injury. Barbara Joan was only fifteen months old and was never to know her father. But he had known his daughter, loving her dearly. It is said that he would show off pictures of her with great pride to anyone who would look. Emanuel's death not only brought psychological and mental torture for Diana, not the least because of its cruel and premature timing – he was only thirty-four at the time of his death – but in practical terms it meant the instant loss of the family provider. A small pension was short measure against a teacher's regular pay and as Diana continued to mourn his loss, spending hours alone in dark despair, she fitfully grappled with the financial void which beset her as a young widow. There was little left with which to indulge Barbara and the child's first doll was said to have been a hot-water bottle.

Diana's family rallied support, her brother reportedly helping out from his meagre army pay when he could and her parents welcoming her and the children into their home nearby as she gave up the apartment she had shared with Emanuel. Diana was intelligent, had been particularly bright as a schoolgirl, and now was able to get a job as a bookkeeper to become the family wage-earner, leaving baby Barbara and brother Sheldon with her parents. Until she was seven Barbara was virtually brought up by her elderly grandmother.

As she grew to realize and mourn her loss Barbara seemed increasingly to resent not having a father. It made her different from the other children and a mixed set of emotions jostled in her mind as she battled to come to terms with her situation. While not having a father made her at times feel somehow special, like having a disability which picked her out from the crowd, more often she felt angry, deprived, cheated and resentful. She pointed out years later that there is a big gap for a young girl growing up without a father. 'I wanted to know why it happened to me; why couldn't I be like other little girls whose fathers came home. My father never came home.'

She never really conquered what she felt subconsciously to be an appalling injustice in not ever knowing her father. She was left to build up a picture from family snapshots, conversations with her mother, glimpses of a man who had been so well liked, respected and admired among friends and colleagues. But it was never enough and as a child she overcompensated for the one loss she could do nothing about by, in her own words, '... feeling more, sensing more, wanting more'. Years later it was the deep affection for her father's memory which was to drive her forward in her profound dedication to the *Yentl* film project. But for the moment the logic that could be expected to develop with the sensibilities of an adult wasn't there to help. She was left with her fantasies about her father, her pride in and love for him becoming the most important thing in her life, filling the empty hours she spent with her grandparents as her mother left for work every day. She grew up withdrawn, inhibited and refused to eat in order to gain attention, though she would cunningly devour sausages and other forbidden tit-bits denied to her at home from friendly non-Jewish neighbours unable to resist the appeal of the scrawny, waif-like youngster. At five Barbara was thin and possibly anaemic. In desperation, thinking it would help to improve her health and be good for her psychologically, her mother packed her off to summer camp. Barbara hated it ... and when her mother tried the same tactic the next year, Barbara was so desperately miserable that she had to be brought home ahead of time.

Born a fretful baby, with no hair and a larger-than-normal head, she later was not a pretty child, her somewhat bland features gaining nothing from the merest suggestion of a cast in one of her eyes. Nor did she mix easily, being more at ease playing on her own. She was already developing into a clever mimic and could sing well, squatting on the doorstep giving impressions of her favourite popular singers of the day. Her mother's decision to remarry in 1949, when Barbara was seven, sadly increased her feeling of isolation. It seemed to her an act of betrayal to the memory of her father. Furthermore she didn't in the beginning or ever take to her stepfather, Louis Kind. His business was in property, but Barbara would demeaningly label him 'a used car salesman or something', when she was older.

The marriage meant a further upheaval. Barbara and her brother were uprooted from their grandparents' care as Louis Kind and Diana moved into a better though not over-large apartment, at the junction of Nostrand and Newkirk Avenues, taking the children with them. Here Barbara slept on a bed-couch in the living-room of the cramped home. If things could have been different these changes might have encouraged a process of emotional stability for Barbara. But her relationship with her stepfather was never to improve, and the new apartment which Louis had provided was always compared unfavourably by Barbara with their original family home. Realistically they were now better off than as a one-parent family, but against many other families in the district, the Kinds didn't have much money to spare for the extras in life.

In an effort to escape from the unhappiness she felt at home, Barbara increasingly preferred the drab atmosphere of outdoors Brooklyn in the early post-war years, but even on the streets among her contemporaries, she discovered little charity or understanding. She couldn't get on with the other children. They taunted her about the way she looked and her unfriendly demeanour. In a *Playboy* interview years later she said that as a nine-year-old other girls would make her cry and run away by making fun of her. She became depressed and isolated. Diana worried about her, particularly since she still rejected much of her food. There was one reported moment of tenderness when her mother, desperate at Barbara's refusal to eat, cuddled her, took her to bed and spoon-fed her. Barbara responded, happy with the attention she was getting, and ate her food with relish.

That episode has been told before, as too the story that, despite Barbara's lack of response, Louis Kind did try hard to break down the barriers which existed between them. But against the verdict that probably Barbara had nothing against him personally, was her later unyielding judgement that he abused her during those years, not physically, but emotionally through a lack of understanding of her presence and being as an individual. It was an inevitable situation, however, which she found impossible to take. This man was taking her father's place … yet how could he? She might well have understood her mother's need, but for her it was out of the question.

It was about this time that she began to experience buzzing in her ears, a condition which was to lead within two or three years to a persistent ringing undertone and a medical diagnosis that she had tinnitus, a condition which was to remain with her. To try to get rid of the noise, Barbara would tie a scarf over her head and round her ears – a tactic, not surprisingly in the humidity of a blistering New York summer, laughed at by the neighbourhood kids on the street; but as an adult she would take the condition for granted and rarely mention it.

While as a young schoolgirl she had a tough time making and

retaining relationships, she applied her mind to classwork, performing well academically, and out of school she found consolation in play-acting which gave her the attention she wanted but found hard to find in normal friendships. As a pupil at Erasmus Hall High School, proud of its status as the oldest secondary school in the USA, her commitment gave no cause for concern and she was happy to study after school to fill in the time, working at her books in the evenings and visiting the local library at weekends. She was very much a loner, shunning the cliques fashionable at school, reportedly strange and Bohemian long before it became the vogue. A classmate from 1959 remembers the seventeen-year-old Barbara being different, wearing purple lipstick, green nail varnish and sandals. 'No one wore sandals then,' she remembers.

She was about eleven when she first discovered movies, being addicted to fan magazines and hypnotically drawn to Loew's King's Theater on nearby Flatbush Avenue. It was there, for just a quarter, that she was first transfixed by the silver screen's glossy heroes and heroines. In the darkened auditorium, alone with her secret thoughts and fantasies, she would identify with the characters portrayed by the likes of Greer Garson, Elizabeth Taylor, Ava Gardner, Joan Crawford, Rita Hayworth, Lana Turner, Jean Simmons and others. Picture-going became a ritual and the certain escape to a new life in which she took over the starring role, being wanted, pursued and in the end, surrendering to the demands of celluloid gods like Victor Mature, Marlon Brando, William Holden and Robert Taylor.

Barbara would act out her scenarios in front of a mirror in the privacy of her bedroom, mimicking facial expressions and trying to capture the emotion of a particular scene she had memorized. When her bedroom or the bathroom became too restrictive she would go up to the roof of the apartment where, without fear of being seen or interrupted, she would shed her inhibitions and throw herself totally into her role playing. Although it is documented that she had made her first public appearance when she was seven, singing at a local parent–teacher association meeting and was later to follow the tradition of young girls in wanting to become a ballerina, until her mother stopped her going to dance classes because she seemed so frail, it was at about this time that she first began to think about what it might be like to be an actress.

Her mother was, like most mothers of sub-teen and early teenage daughters, worried, not only over the frequency of her visits to the movies, but even more by the influence they were having on her daughter. She saw with concern the way the glamorous make-believe world of films was beginning to dislodge the realities of life and exhorted her to forget her fantasies. It wasn't too early to begin thinking about what sort of job she would like when she left school, urged her mother. Diana had visions of her becoming a school clerk, as once she herself had been, and bought her a typewriter so that she could expand her skills in readiness for a 'real career'.

But in the intervening years, nothing had happened to encourage Barbara to settle down with a firmer grip on her emotions. Despite the fraught relationship with her stepfather, Barbara had taken no pleasure in the growing deterioration of her mother's second marriage, least of all when she and Louis decided to separate. That was in 1954 when Barbara was twelve. The couple were never to be divorced (he died in 1970), but their union had produced a daughter in 1951. As Diana decided once more to find a job to help make ends meet, Barbara, the house now clear of Louis, would happily baby-sit her half-sister, Rosalind, singing quietly to her to keep her amused. Years later, when Streisand was a big star, she was delighted to see the progress of Rosalind's own professional singing career and the two of them, with their mother, became friends.

But at the time and despite her mother's advice and exhortation, the desire to become an actress was taking hold in Barbara's mind. The notion took a major step forward when, in 1956 as an impressionable fourteen-year-old, she was taken one Saturday afternoon to the Cort Theater on Broadway to see *The Diary of Anne Frank*. For the starry-eyed youngster a visit to the theatre on Broadway was excitement enough, but the impact of that particular play was to make the whole experience significant in its inspirational intensity. Barbara saw clearly in the story of the world classic, parallels with her own life, reading into the experience a significance and meaning which perhaps only she cared to identify. Barbara grasped the experience hungrily and intuitively as a positive signal to her own career, reinforcing her single-mindedness to become an actress whatever happened.

The thought horrified her mother. Born into the traditional

Jewish ethic of the times, where a woman's place was in the home with a firm adherence to the structured traditions of the faith, Diana was unable to call on any family background of professional show business to cushion what she feared to be the implications of her daughter's ambitions to go into the theatre. That aside, Diana was anxious because she could see nothing other than heartache and disappointment if Barbara peristed. Even allowing for the propensity which mothers instinctively have for their offspring, it could hardly be said that Barbara gave signs of developing into the classic mould of the stage heroine. Still of an age when she lacked the character to make up for her absence of traditonal prettiness, Barbara was doomed to fail, considered her mother. But it was becoming increasingly clear to Diana, despite what she thought at first to be her daughter's infatuation with the idea of acting, that Barbara's crazy idea could no longer be dismissed as a passing fad. By the time she was fifteen, in 1957, she had made up her mind; and her mother knew it.

If at that time Diana looked for some consolation, it would be in Barbara's continued abilities academically. She was by no means a duffer. She worked hard, studied conscientiously, and in January 1959, when she was approaching seventeen, she graduated from Erasmus Hall High with excellent standards. By then, though, she had already opposed her mother on two significant occasions. The first time was in 1957 when Barbara wanted to use the $150 she had inherited from her grandfather for the enrolment fee for the Malden Bridge Summer Theater near Albany in upstate New York. Her mother saw it as wasting money on a whim, but after a long and intense battle, finally gave in, perhaps feeling that this raw experience of the real thing would lay the theatre business to rest once and for all.

Far from it. Barbara was infatuated and enraptured throwing herself with commendable and equal vigour into everything, from scene shifting and stage sweeping to painting, fetching and carrying, and over-acting outrageously in the occasional part she managed to talk them into giving her. It was an unrivalled experience and she was determined to go again the following summer. To be fair to Mrs Streisand, once she had seen how determined Barbara was to go to Malden Bridge the first time, she had told her to keep the $150 and instead financed her, giving her $300. She had dearly wanted Barbara to accompany herself and Barbara's half-sister on a family holiday, but, as Mrs Streisand was to explain later, once she knew her daughter would be happier doing what she wanted, she gave in.

To help pay for her second visit to the Malden Bridge Summer Theater, Barbara started helping out at Choy's Chinese Restaurant on Newkirk Avenue close to her home, first as a waitress and then as a cashier. She had known the Choys since she began baby-sitting for them when she was about twelve and was to build up a close relationship, particularly with Muriel Choy, who became a kind of second mother to her. Barbara was still at Erasmus Hall High at this point and often, as any young teenager, would find it easier to talk to Muriel rather than her own mother about the more intimate side of life. As a loner Barbara also found both consolation and strength in the sharing of a kind of ethnic minority status with the Choys, who continued to have very fond memories of Barbara long after the restaurant closed down and they had moved to a more fashionable area north of Flatbush.

It is also likely that they, not being personally involved and able to form a more detached judgement, could more readily see why Barbara wanted so desperately for her mother to give up the home in Brooklyn and take an apartment in Manhattan. But her mother, placing as much emphasis on security and 'a normal life' for her daughter as Barbara was doing on becoming an actress and in the neon-lighted attractions of the theatre land, strongly resisted all her daughter's arguments, even when Barbara, exasperated, told her: 'But Ma, you can get an apartment there for only $105 – why can't we afford it?'

In the meantime a second job as an usherette at a local cinema at weekends brought her closer to the kind of life she craved for. After going back to Malden Bridge for a second term, during which she showed enthusiastic if undisciplined promise in minor roles in *Picnic* and *The Desk Set*, where she played the office flirt with eyebrow-raising abandon, and gaining her impressive graduation six months early with an average grade of ninety three, she was all set to deliver her ultimatum: if the family wouldn't move to Manhattan, she would go to live there on her own.

Mrs Streisand knew her daughter well enough to know that she wasn't bluffing. She also realized that any kind of heavy-handed parental control was doomed to fail, for Barbara was now old enough to begin to make her own way in the world. Since graduation she had worked in Manhattan as a switchboard operator and had been saving every cent she could. She had honoured her mother's wishes to get a good education and now was ready and determined to spread her wings, to fulfil her ambitions of becoming an actress. Mrs Streisand confined her involvement to approving Barbara's prospective flatmate.

That first shared flat of Barbara's was on Thirty-fourth Street and, tiny as it was, it gave Barbara her first real independence. But much more important to living in Manhattan was the passion she displayed for acting lessons after she had signed up with two coaches. She had already chosen her stage name – Angelina Scarangella – lifted at random from a Manhattan telephone directory. Barbara loved the sense of freedom which living away from her mother gave her. She fully committed herself to her career and was thrilled when both her drama coaches told her she had enough potential to start going in for auditions for real parts.

The disappointment at doing just that, however, was devastating. They always wanted someone with experience, indicated Barbra later when recalling those times. But how was she to gain the experience which appeared to be so vital if nobody would give her a start? It is a classic situation that many job-hunters face, not only in theatre. It infuriated Barbara who reportedly found it degrading and humiliating. 'Nobody should be forced to beg for work,' she said. Yet, devoid of an acting pedigree, could she really expect to impress hard-nosed casting directors who saw little in her general appearance to capture their interest? Even then she was fiercely uncompromising, combatant, defiant almost, and although she was always to deny strongly that she dressed in way-out fashions, she was inclined to wear an assortment of garments which collectively bordered on the beatnik. And if she was noted for her facial appearance, it was for the wrong reasons – an absence of traditional classic features and perhaps looking a little too ethnic.

It was difficult to balance the need to earn with the insistent demands of her ambition. She had a number of jobs, was out of work for a time and forfeited her unemployment benefit when it was discovered that instead of going for a traditional job interview, she had spent the time trying to get a part in a play. She battled against the system, refusing to have her nose fixed and to pretty herself up with better make-up and a simpler dress. Why should she? She was Barbara Joan Streisand and they should take her as she was. She would make it as her own person.

She applied the same strong views to her singing. Her voice was good and if she lacked experience and technique, the potential was enough to attract the interest of people who could have helped her break into show business. But she didn't want to be a singer. She wanted to be an actress.

For a while the situation seemed a deadlock, but she was proud as well as stubborn, refusing, according to her stepfather, all offers of help. She would still take in the food brought to her occasionally by her mother, but for anything else was determined to make her own way forward. The future began to look bleak, but fate was soon to move in Barbara's favour. Within months she would meet the first person to have a profound influence on her career; take her first though unsteady steps on stage; win a significant talent contest as a singer and gain her first professional singing engagement; and change her name. Within a couple of years, by 1962, Barbra Streisand would become Broadway's most acclaimed new talent. And while still remarkably inexperienced for such a phenomenal part, she would be chosen for the role of Fanny Brice in *Funny Girl*, which opened on Broadway on 26 March 1964.

But, as she struggled to find a first footing in entertainment, back in her latest small flat on West Forty-eighth Street, and with no job and career prospects gloomy, it was her flatmate, Marilyn Fried, who set the ball rolling. She happened to overhear Barbara sing, was impressed by what she heard, and told her that she must try singing. Barbara stuck to her ambition to be an actress, but did go along for an audition for *The Sound of Music*. She wasn't chosen, but she impressed Eddie Blum of the Rodgers and Hammerstein casting office who did a lot to convince her that she was good enough to be a great singer one day.

Meanwhile, and with the help of a young designer called Terry Leong who smoothed out and toned down her appearance, she managed to get cast in *The Insect Comedy*, which James Spada in his excellent biography of Streisand described as a 'makeshift production "slapped together" by a group of out-of-work actors'. Barbara played four parts, the show lasted just three nights, but the experience brought her into contact with a talented young actor called Barry Dennen. They talked together, swapped stories and ambitions. After hearing Barbara sing through his own domestic, yet sophisticated recording equipment, Dennen, whose personal collection included tapes and records of some of America's finest female singers like Billie Holiday, Helen Morgan and Lee Wiley, insisted that she should try to make her break through singing. Barbara was still unsure, but by this time she had become attracted to Dennen, later moving into his apartment, and was more predisposed to take note of what he recommended.

But she didn't give in without a fight and Dennen in the end, playing it cool, struck a bargain. He persuaded her to enter the Thursday-night talent contest at the Lion club nearby and his side of the deal was to work with her in selecting songs and generally developing a professional presentation. The club was for gays, but what was more important to Barbara was that if she won she would be booked into The Lion at $50 a week and as much free food as she could eat.

It was too tempting but, ever the perfectionist, she agreed only after arranging a 'dummy run' before a few friends in Dennen's flat. As Donald Zec and Anthony Fowles in their book *Barbra, A Biography of Barbra Streisand*, explain: 'She decided to arrange her own pre-contest audition, not in a theater, not in a recording studio, but in her kitchen. Even there she was too nervous to face the handful of friends gathered to give her moral support. [Perhaps especially the handful of friends – how many potential talents shrivel under this too-personal scrutiny?] She turned her back on them. Fixing her gaze on the calendar on the wall, she sang the subtle, musically complex 'A Sleeping Bee'. She finished. And waited. There was no applause, no comment. "Well, am I any good?" she was forced to ask. Still nothing. "I remember, when I turned around," she recalled later, "I couldn't understand why they had tears in their eyes".'

The reaction was similarly electrifying when she faced the audience at The Lion. The history of talent contests gives audiences few marks for attentiveness or the wit to respond appreciatively to a gifted performer. Acts at The Lion tended to fare no better on talent night and perhaps who could blame them because not always did the standard of performance on such occasions demand, or indeed deserve, their undivided attention. But exceptions there are – and Barbara's début there was such.

Panicked to her bones in front of such a potentially wayward audience, with all the self-doubts of an inexperienced performer just past her eighteenth birthday, Barbara's plain looks and eccentric appearance, topped by her duotone hair, were quickly set aside by her all-male audience. She eased herself into the Harold Arlen, Truman Capote ballad she had 'auditioned' to her private audience of friends in the secrecy of her home. What a well-chosen vehicle to showcase Barbara's remarkable vocal talent it proved to be – the sensitivity, the tonal quality, the ease of execution through the scale, the controlled excitement and inspirational quality of her delivery. The fidgeting and gossiping stopped as the audience's attention was drawn hypnotically to the young girl, vulnerably alone on the stage with only the accompanying piano for support, her voice and interpretation hugely transcending the usual offerings from the stage on talent-spotting nights.

The audience was spellbound, anxious to know more about this new talent. The contest was never really a contest. Barbara won her engagement and free meals and reportedly celebrated her first major success by walking barefoot in Central Park. Whether she liked it or not, it had been proved beyond doubt that she was a singer – though she continued through her professional career to remain loyal to her early protestations that she was an actress first.

News of Barbara's devastating impact on stage spread widely and rapidly. People lined up to crowd in to see her act. It was the first glimmer of what was to develop into a Streisand cult within just a few years. Barbara was retained at The Lion for a second and then a third week, at the same time working closely with Barry Dennen on the next stage of what they both now confidently looked forward to as her singing career. She worked hard on the tough regime of building up a professional act which Dennen had specified. He worked with her, guiding, advising, encouraging, pointing her in the right direction. Her confidence in front of an audience improved while performing at The Lion. She was able to relax more. Her enraptured audiences were building her reputation and were soon to earn her an audition at the nearby Bon Soir nightclub. More sophisticated than The Lion and a more conventional nightclub, the Bon Soir would raise her status and place her more securely in the show-business spotlight, even if she was engaged following her successful audition as a warm-up for top-of-the-bill Phyllis Diller. Barbara rejoiced in the two-week engagement and the $108 a week was more than double what she had received at The Lion.

The little girl from Pulaski Street might well have thought that her secret dreams were perhaps about to come true, for her two-weeks engagement was to be extended to eleven, and her fee increased. Significantly, too, she was building her reputation on a new name. Gone for ever was Angelina Scarangella and in a successful attempt to give more fluency to her own name she crossed out Joan and an 'a' from Barbara. As Barbra Streisand she began to feel just a little that she was perhaps now solidly established in show business ... and on her way to becoming the actress she had always wanted to be.

3 'I Want to be an Actress'

No one person discovered Barbra Streisand, but Barry Dennen well might claim that he at least planted her feet firmly on the road to stardom. With tact and understanding, and just a touch of subtle deception, he was able to convince her that the best way of achieving her ambitions as an actress was to exploit her obvious talent as a singer. He persuaded her that the art of putting across a song, by definition, incorporated the principles of acting. Without that her obstinacy in wanting to act rather than sing would certainly have impeded the development of her career at that time.

Someone else who had a hand in the construction of Barbra Streisand, superstar in the making, was a friend of Dennen's called Bob Schulenberg. He came into her life during those early days at the Bon Soir. When he first called to see Dennen from his family home in California, Barbra was not the most subdued of dressers. Colour co-ordination didn't have a high priority in her wardrobe. To be fair she'd had little time or money to indulge herself in fineries, buying most of her clothes from thrift shops. 'I wore secondhand clothes,' she told Britain's David Jacobs. 'I had a theory – the people who donate their clothes to thrift shops must be rich, so therefore they must be clean – I mean, they must take baths.' Not yet nineteen when she met Schulenberg she dressed in what she considered to be the rage of the moment, mixing styles and colours indiscriminately, provocatively hoisting her hemline above the knee before the 'Swinging Sixties' made it fashionably acceptable to do so. She dressed to please herself and she liked to shock.

31

For a time Dennen and Schulenberg worked on Barbra to create the kind of transformation of which Professor Higgins could have been proud. In the way Dennen was able to change her attitude towards her act and stage presentation, Schulenberg concentrated on her personal appearance. He has talked about the shock of his first meeting with her: as he and Dennen were walking down Sixth Avenue in New York he saw this apparition coming towards them. She had two shopping bags to each hand and sprouting out of them were feathers, sequins, net, all sorts of accessory stuff, lots of it. She was like a whole studio on wheels, he told author Rene Jordan. 'She had a band of hair across her forehead and a hairpiece pinned on top of her head ... she had wisps of eyeliner and darkened eyelids under her brows ... her wide and generous mouth was accentuated with mahogany–purple lipstick and her earrings were glass balls that seemed to hang all the way down to her thorax.'

Barbra was always a good and steady talker, and asked a lot of questions. Schulenberg, who was to become a professional illustrator but was then job-hunting in New York, was captivated after Dennen had introduced them and the two struck up a friendship. Because of his feeling for art and the harmonies of life he could see the outstanding potential in Barbra and just how striking she could become with more attention to her make-up, hair styling, and the presentation of herself as a complete person. He indulged himself, applying cosmetics carefully to trim away the pudginess of her cheeks and to emphasize the striking bone structure. He gave her hair body and style. The transformation process was stunning and she became a head-turner for the right reasons rather than the wrong. Barbra at eighteen was captivating, full of unspoilt fun and naturally energetic and friendly. Although she and Schulenberg became very close friends, there was never any romance between them.

Recognizing and contributing to the development of an early talent is one thing, being able to exploit and project that talent commercially is another. While Barry Dennen and Bob Schulenberg undoubtedly warrant their key places in any story of Streisand, it was the promising theatrical agent Marty Erlichman who next stepped into the frame. For it was his perception, contacts, skill, timing and intuition which was to be so crucial in elevating Barbra Streisand to international superstar status.

Erlichman, hearing about the way Barbra was captivating her nightclub audiences, went to see her act, visited her backstage and asked if he could represent her. It so happened that she was becoming disillusioned with her then agent who, she was to say later, wanted her to sing more 'popular' songs, get her nose fixed and change her name.

The story is that Barbra asked Erlichman if he wanted to change anything about her and when he said he didn't, she asked him to take over. She asked him to try to arrange something for her in the theatre and before long this led her to a forthcoming revue called *Another Evening with Harry Stoones*. This collection of musical and comic sketches was approaching its opening at the Gramercy Arts Theater in Greenwich Village, and had been fully cast when an unexpected vacancy arose. Barbra was one of three who auditioned for the part and after two auditions was taken on.

After numerous previews the show opened on 21 October 1961 and, sadly for all concerned, closed the same day, victim of killing notices in both the *New York Times* and *Herald Tribune*. The show itself, ambitious though it might have been in concept and capably put across – and boosted by having singer-actress and Broadway success Diana Sands in the cast, none the less proved too cynical and 'fringe' for the times. It was conceived as a satire on the then tedious, seemingly unending *An Evening With ...* shows. Sketches made fun of just about everything. Good notices later in the week failed to save such a thinly financed show in a period when critics on the major papers carried enormous influence and power.

Barbra was devastated to be out of work again, just when it seemed that she was beginning to build a name and attract attention, for her own personal notices had been good. She had appeared in nine of the show's cumbersome cavalcade of thirty-eight sketches, three of them as a featured solo singer. She was noted by *Variety*, among others, as a future vocal prospect and a 'slim, offbeat, deadpan comedienne with an excellent flair for dropping a dour blackout gag...'.

But, despite this unfortunate début as Streisand's manager, Marty Erlichman was to remain a powerful influence on her career. Her potential and success would soon dictate that he relinquish all other clients in order to concentrate fully on her

personal representation, and in the end he was to remain with
Barbra for some fifteen years.

Similarly enduring was her friendship with Bob Schulenberg,
but during a turbulent though fragmentarily successful time
leading up to *Harry Stoones* her affair with Barry Dennen had not
survived, though at one time they had talked about marriage. It
seems, according to Schulenberg's observations, that Dennen's
respect for Barbra was not what it had been and he began to take
her for granted, not calling her when he might have done when
away from their apartment on business trips. It was Barbra and
Schulenberg who had innocently angered Dennen by being so
involved in working out a new make-up style together, and
having so much fun doing it, that they failed to keep a date with
Dennen. He never seemed to forget it ... while years later Barbra
it appears hadn't forgiven him, their relationship as and when
their paths crossed, being extremely tepid. But in those
friendlier days in New York, the story goes that Dennen at one
time was more than a week late from a trip to California to see
his parents, but didn't bother to telephone Barbra, who had
planned an elaborate homecoming on the expected day of his
return. There was little doubt that Dennen had lost much of
what he had once felt for her and his growing neglect and lack
of consideration led to the breakup. An engagement which took
Barbra out of New York for a spell ended their relationship.

It wasn't the only set-back during this period. After packing a
bed-roll and moving out of Dennen's flat, Barbra tried to control
her career while moving haphazardly from one place to another,
taking advantage of friends and associates who would offer to
put her up for a night or two. Literally 'of no fixed abode' for a
spell, after being evicted from her apartment, managers, agents,
production and contact men were driven out of their minds
trying to get hold of her and thanked providence when she
finally slumped into a $62.70-a-month rent-controlled apartment
on Third Avenue and Sixty-sixth Street.

Barbra's already precarious financial state had been considerably compromised by the threat of legal action by her former
agent, Ted Rozar, who was making life difficult for her because
of her switch to Erlichman. Although Barbra never discussed
the outcome, a figure of around $5,000, a lot for those times for
someone yet to make the big break, has been talked about by
insiders as the price it cost her to settle the dispute.

These issues apart, Barbra had been reasonably satisfied with the way her career had been developing up to the collapse of *Harry Stoones*. Early in 1961 she had been called back for a second stint at the Bon Soir and this time, more confident and mature as an entertainer, she made considerable impact. It was while she was resident at the Bon Soir that she made her television début, on 5 April 1961, as a guest on the *Jack Paar Show* with Phyllis Diller, who had recommended her, and if she didn't gain overnight stardom, she did enough to later gain a singing audition for the new talk show, *PM East*.

Barbra had continued to have a capacious appetite for success and had made sure that no experience had been wasted. Her first appearance on *PM East* was well received. They liked her singing, her personality and presence before the camera. They liked the fact that she was no stereotype. She was enough of an off-beat to help the programme gain a strong focus and during the summer of 1961 she made repeated appearances on *PM East*. They liked her wit, her singing of course, her uncompromising views expressed openly and honestly. And her looks were so individual that they gave the show a distinct identity.

Her success at the Bon Soir led to an engagement at The Blue Angel. She had auditioned before the opening (and closing!) of *Harry Stoones*, and her engagement at this highly rated night spot which attracted many of the show-business élite helped to make up for her disappointment at the shock closure of the off-Broadway show. The Blue Angel had been the launch pad for a string of top stars, the most notable perhaps being Harry Belafonte. Could it provide a similar springboard for Barbra? But at the start, that wasn't the issue. The Blue Angel was the top of its class and was noted for featuring established stars. To the management there Streisand's engagement was something of a gamble and, although she had gained some minor status, she was still to be closely watched. She was unconventional as a singer; still likely to be unorthodox and imprecisely disciplined as an act.

But there is no doubt that Barbra's engagements at The Blue Angel had a significant impact on her career curve. It surged significantly while she was there, first in her conquest of New York's nightclub scene, then when she secured against all odds a key role in *I Can Get it for You Wholesale*; and finally for her rave reviews from key critics for this, her Broadway début.

The world's greatest optimist would have been hard pressed to give Barbra a chance when she turned up at auditions for *Wholesale*. For one thing she had been singing at The Blue Angel until 2 a.m. and had then feasted herself on a comprehensive Thanksgiving dinner until 4.30, despite a scheduled 10 a.m. audition. More significantly, there just wasn't a part in the show that she could reasonably be expected to play. But credit director Arthur Laurents with the ability to see beyond the obvious. The only possible role for Streisand was that of Miss Marmelstein, a 50-year-old hard-done-by spinster secretary never likely, in her view, to rate with the opposite sex and destined always to suffer the sexual indignity of being addressed as Miss Marmelstein. Laurents, who would later make his mark with successful stage musicals like *West Side Story* and *Gypsy*, however, was so impressed by Barbra's unconventional attraction and so utterly captivated by her outstanding vocal talent that he was determined to have her in the show.

Barbra, for her part, followed her instincts at the audition by making sure she stood out from the rest of the girls. She wore a big fur coat which she insisted on keeping round her during the audition, and brought a huge pile of music which she plonked on top of the piano, spreading it across the stage as she walked away. It was a crude device to make her stand out from the rest, and typically Streisand. Much later Barbra insisted she didn't wear the old coat on purpose. 'It was my old coat, a favourite old coat and right for the character, so I wore it,' she explained. But for Arthur Laurents she needn't have bothered. When she began to sing, that was more than enough. Laurents said later as reported by James Spada: 'I was determined to have this girl in the show. Not only was she a marvellous singer, but there was something unconventional about her. I thought I could take advantage of her unusual looks.'

So resolute was Laurents that he was able to convince everyone who mattered, including the authors of *Wholesale* and producer David Merrick, that having Barbra Streisand in the show was far more important than maintaining the character rigidly as written. 'The way she looks, she will be accepted as a spinster, and the audience will have no idea of her age,' he said. Thus Barbra Streisand won the part of Yetta Tessye Marmelstein, and if she felt it to be a little too ethnic for total comfort, it was to be an important marker in an ascending career. Merrick, incidentally, was to be otherwise significant in Streisand's climb to international stardom.

The show itself was hardly an outrageous success. After trial performances in Philadelphia and Boston, it opened at the Shubert Theater on Broadway on 22 March 1962 and was closed within the year. But that was more than long enough for Streisand to have created an enormous impact and a huge following. While those first reviews for the show were disturbingly mixed, there was hardly a critic who didn't acclaim her personally as a major new talent.

Opening night was a dazzling experience for Barbra. Her Miss Marmelstein number, written by Jerome Weidman with lyrics by Harold Rome, then known for revues but who was later to emerge into full-scale musicals, was never going to make it as a long-life standard, but Barbra's attacking interpretation of a plain-Jane Jewish spinster's lack of even elementary success with the opposite sex made sure it was the one number in the show that audiences would remember. Her knock-kneed, pigeon-toed interpretation as Yetta Tessye Marmelstein, denied the love success she so desperately sought, highlighted her talent as a natural comedienne and among rave notices she received, the *Morning Telegraph*'s Whitney Bolton declared that at nineteen years of age she had packed thirty-eight years of poise and professionalism into her young life. 'Miss Streisand, singing or talking, burbling or walking, screaming or whispering, is a great, good friend to *I Can Get it for You Wholesale*,' he added.

The show was significant in two other ways, both supplementary in terms of Streisand's career, but none the less interesting: one personal, the other amusing as a side issue to Barbra's professional background. Making his Broadway début along with Barbra in *Wholesale* was a handsome young chorus member from the show *Irma La Douce* called Elliott Gould. Elliott went for the lead role of Harry Bogen, an unabashed go-getter in the fashion industry who doesn't hesitate to use people or bend the rules to make his mark in the business. He met Streisand for the first time at one of the four auditions she attended for the Miss Marmelstein role. An innocent move by Barbra gave romance the chance to blossom.

She had just had a telephone installed in her modest flat

above Oscar's fish restaurant, close to the studio where the *PM East* television programme in which she was now a regular, was taped, and after doing her audition, she began handing out slips of paper which included her new telephone number and a message inviting someone to call her. Somehow Elliott didn't get one, but managed to intercept a slip which was being discarded. That evening just one person took Barbra up on her invitation. The telephone rang and when she answered it Elliott said: 'You asked for someone to call you, so I called.' He said he thought she had been brilliant at the audition and, before hanging up, said: 'This is Elliott Gould.'

It might have ended there ... but didn't. They quickly became attracted to each other. Both were young, Barbra still nineteen and Elliott 22, and their romance blossomed during walks across New York before and after performances, visits to Rockefeller Plaza, playful snow fights and light affectionate kisses innocently stolen. There had been no one for Barbra since Barry Dennen and she was happy enough as the romance developed and intensified. Elliott went on record later: 'I found her absolutely exquisite.' He was fascinated by her and thought she was beautiful, like a flower. They spent a lot of time together, eating pop-corn, visiting restaurants, bars and movie houses for the late performances, and it cannot have surprised many people when Elliott moved in with her. They were later to be married, but many years on, long after they had separated, Gould admitted to authors Donald Zec and Anthony Fowles: 'I must admit that the happiest memories I have of Barbra are when we were living together before we were married. We were very dependent on each other then. We lived together, not for any legal reason.'

But if their careers had brought them together, it was equally their careers which were eventually to separate them. Although Gould had secured the male lead in *Wholesale*, the part did not provide the possibilities which might have led to the kind of career breakthrough that Barbra was able to achieve through her role as Miss Marmelstein. More significantly, as Barbra's reputation soared after *Wholesale*, Elliott's foundered. He was later to make a strong impact in a couple of notable pictures, but at the time the different trajectory of their respective careers would begin to eat into their relationship and in the ensuing years as Barbra began to establish herself as the greatest female entertainer in the world, the gulf between them was to widen. The spark had long since disappeared when they separated in February 1969.

Going back to *Wholesale*, an amusing side issue was Barbra's background notes which she concocted for the official programme of the show. Her biographical detail indicated that she had been born in Madagascar and brought up in Rangoon before being educated at the Erasmus Hall High School in Brooklyn. Barbra was unabashed when admitting that she made it up to gain attention. She considered it quite normal to exaggerate almost to any degree and, for later additions of the programme, replaced Madagascar and Rangoon with Zanzibar and Aruba, before admitting to the more prosaic truth of the matter. But by that time she was such a success that it didn't matter.

4 Broadway Triumph for Stage-struck Barbra

Barbra Streisand's first major album was released in late February 1963, but it had been a long haul to persuade Columbia, or any other record company for that matter, of her potential as a recording artist. Barbra was desperate to make the breakthrough and had insisted from the start that Marty Erlichman should apply his energies and influence to securing a record deal. That is where the big reputations were to be made, on record, and dramatically overnight in many cases, Streisand thought. But Columbia and others held back. The trouble was the difficulty in trying to pigeon-hole Barbra. She wasn't a swinger, couldn't claim to be jazz-inspired, was outside the popular rock 'n' roll scene, didn't really identify with the female ballad singers of the day; nor did her voice project 'theatre' or 'stage' exclusively enough.

Barbra in voice, as in every other facet of her being and personality, was her own person. She was so individual she scared every record producer Erlichman talked to. Every record company in the business turned her down. Erlichman battled on Barbra's behalf for nine months without success. Even the boss of Columbia Records, Goddard Lieberson, was blind to Barbra's enormous potential. When Marty managed to persuade him to listen to her sing he thought he was home and dry. But the verdict came back: she's too special to generate a mass following.

Paradoxically it was to be Lieberson, looking at Barbra for a second time and against what he considered to be his better judgement, who opened the way to Streisand's massively successful recording career. But there was no dramatic breakthrough. It emerged slowly, steadily, almost imperceptibly, before the explosion occurred.

Curiously, too, it was Columbia who almost inadvertently set the process in motion, for it was their original cast recording of *Wholesale* which marked Barbra's début on record. As in the show, her 'Miss Marmelstein' number was the highlight of the album and a short time after she was remembered by *Wholesale* composer Harold Rome, who was then turning his attention to a new album to celebrate the twenty-fifth anniversary of his outstanding Broadway hit, *Pins and Needles*. Against much advice Rome insisted on featuring Barbra on the new album, mainly because of her enormous if surprising success as Miss Marmelstein, and she took her chance comprehensively. She sang six numbers, two of which particularly received good critical acclaim and John F. Indcox of *High Fidelity* was nearer the mark than he can have possibly supposed when he reported: 'Here Miss Streisand sounds very much like a young Fanny Brice.' A prophetic statement indeed.

Without losing her individuality, without sacrificing the eccentricities which made her Streisand, Barbra was now beginning to command attention. Her earlier impact at the Bon Soir had cleared the way for her to get into television and her increasing popularity in this high-profile media, combined with her success on the *Wholesale* and *Pins and Needles* albums, transformed Barbra Streisand into a much more marketable package.

When Columbia's Goddard Lieberson was urged once more to take notice of this rapidly rising young star, he listened, looked and this time was willing to take a chance. He signed her to a record contract, but still was not in the least confident that he had even now made the correct decision. He would have plenty of time to reflect and muse on the doubts he held about Barbra at that time. For it was early 1963 when he added his signature to the Streisand contract and in that same year she crashed through the show-biz barrier with devastating impact. Not only did she make enormously significant albums for Columbia that same year, but also in 1963 she was selected female vocalist of the year, was one of the hottest properties on television with offers to appear as a guest on all the top coast-to-coast shows, made her début at Las Vegas and was to become the front-runner for the lead in a Broadway show which was not only destined to make theatrical history, but would lead directly to her dramatic breakthrough into movies.

In early 1963 Barbra Streisand had worried that her career seemed to be getting nowhere. She wondered if her successful Miss Marmelstein role had typecast her, prematurely stunting her ambitions. She was being urged by some of the biggest names in the business to change her tactics, to become more orthodox, to make a more obvious appeal to the masses. But Barbra, defiant and determined as ever to make it on her own terms, contemptuously proved that the pundits are not always right. For, given the opportunity, and by resolutely remaining Streisand the individual, she also in 1963 was invited by President Kennedy to sing at the White House press correspondents' dinner; was a triumph on the nightclub circuit and in concert; was invited by established superstar Judy Garland to appear on her weekly television show; made her first brief visit to London; got married – on 13 September; and took in a major nationwide tour. From just $50 two years before, she could now command between $5,000 and $7,000 a week.

Since Elliott Gould had moved into Barbra's apartment things had been going well for the young couple. Though each was individualistic by nature, they would often find consolation in together confronting situations and attitudes which offended them. This had become apparent during their time in *I Can Get it for You Wholesale*, when both sailed close to the wind. At one time they were on the verge of being replaced. It was no secret that Barbra had offended some of the more experienced members of the cast by, as they saw it, making a pitch for the leading man – and she, with no background in the theatre, still an immature teenager, and taking what amounted to what originally had been quite a minor bit part in the show.

Barbra didn't help herself – by simply being herself. Candid views from her contemporaries suggest that she is not at her most comfortable or best when having to submit to a cohesive discipline, and at that stage of course, she had scant experience of such a situation. Drawing from her more solitary role as a nightclub singer, she would at rehearsal and during the pre-Broadway performances instinctively vary and amend the projection of her role, adding nuances and inflections without warning, upsetting and disturbing other members of the cast who were more experienced and disciplined in terms of stage courtesies and etiquette.

Nor, it has been recorded, was her time-keeping as reliable as it might have been. Close associates reveal Barbra's difficulty sometimes in setting her priorities and at one point she seems to have been too preoccupied with the redecoration of her apartment back in New York, which friends were supervising for her, to pay the close attention to time schedules which colleagues expected and deserved. But it is not easy for Barbra to be guided by advice, however well meaning, and as Donald Zec and Anthony Fowles report in *Barbra – A Biography of Barbra Streisand*: 'When Lillian Roth (an experienced actress who took the part of Gould's mother in the show) kindly and perceptively took her to one side and explained that a certain basic professional courtesy would help everyone and her own cause most of all, Barbra was polite but unresponsive.'

In Philadelphia, prior to opening on Broadway, Barbra performed below her potential and it was down to director Arthur Laurents to give her a ticking off before the whole cast. Writer Jerome Weidman and composer and lyricist Harold Rome both feared he may have gone too far, so, while Weidman went over to console Streisand, though it was by no means necessary since she appeared to be more concerned with the layout of her apartment than with the admonition she had just received, Rome tackled Laurents and told him he was sure that Barbra would settle down and be an outstanding success. Producer David Merrick, much to the concern of Rome, had earlier talked about firing Streisand and, according to Laurents, Elliott too because he felt they were unattractive. The assessment was more crucial for Elliott, since he had the male lead, and Laurents has reported that it was only on his insistence that Gould remained, or he himself would resign, that he was still there when the show opened on Broadway.

But the attraction Barbra and Elliott had for one another made this turbulence relatively unimportant to them, though Elliott came out strongly at one point claiming later that he saved Barbra's job. He said he wasn't much concerned with his own career as a performer, but he was determined to save hers. The sentiments, if true, were not misplaced, for Elliott was to see his own future blighted by lack of opportunity and bad luck.

Early in 1963 he managed to secure an important break and flew to London to star as Ozzie in *On the Town* at the Prince of Wales Theatre. Barbra showed her affection by cancelling a couple of important engagements and following him to London for the opening on 26 May. It was Barbra's first trip overseas and she was desperate for Elliott to be a success. Gould gave a creditable performance but the project must have been highly problematical from the start. *On the Town* had been an enormous film success following its release by MGM in 1949 and some years before that had run for two years on Broadway. But after seeing high-profile superstars like Frank Sinatra, Gene Kelly and Jules Munshin cast as the three sailors on leave in New York in the film version, along with Betty Garrett, Ann Miller and Vera-Ellen, could the public be expected to be satisfied with the more restrictive elements of a stage presentation?

Reviews were not optimistic and sadly the show came off after a few weeks. By this time Barbra had returned to the US, leaving Elliott alone to find consolation in London's casino life. When he returned to the United States, depleted financially, it was to a new luxury home which Barbra had acquired on Central Park West, a smart penthouse formerly owned by Lorenz Hart.

But, for Barbra, magical 1963 was taking on a fairy-tale dimension. Her wildest dreams of success couldn't have seriously contemplated anything like this. *The Barbra Streisand Album* had been released in late February and within just two weeks it had made her the premier and best-selling female singer in the United States. The album featured a careful selection of songs from her nightclub presentations and included numbers which were to become Streisand specials like 'Cry Me a River', 'Who's Afraid of the Big, Bad Wolf?' and most significant of all, 'Happy Days Are Here Again'. The latter wasn't really expected to be a blockbuster, but Barbra's incredibly slow-tempo version of the normally rousing Democratic Party's rallying song was an inspiration which paid off and the single version became an enormous hit. It was really Barbra's first standard. Credit for slowing down the tempo goes to Ken Welch, according to James Spada in *Streisand – The Woman and The Legend*, quoting Peter Matz, a conductor – arranger who had been assigned to this first major album of Streisand's because she had been unhappy about some of the arrangements on the earlier album, *Pins and Needles*.

Barbra had asked Harold Rome if he could recommend someone whose ideas would be more in tune with her own and he recommended Matz. Spada reports: 'Peter Matz recalls the genesis of Barbra's unique arrangement: "Doing the song slowly was Ken Welch's idea. He was working on *The Garry Moore Show* when Barbra was a guest, and they used to do a segment on each show called *The Wonderful Year*. On Barbra's show, the year was 1932 or whenever "Happy Days" was a hit, and Barbra was supposed to sing the song. Ken suggested that she sing it slowly and sarcastically, conveying the opposite meaning from what the words were saying, and of course it was incredibly effective. I don't think Ken ever got any credit for that".'

The sarcasm may have drawn the attention of some enthusiasts to the song, but from a musical standpoint it was the slower tempo and the Streisand interpretation which carried it forward to become an early Streisand classic. Even in the 1990s, in an estranged and generally hostile popular music climate, it stands up proudly. The passion of her delivery, the remarkable voice range, the neat change of key halfway through, those consumately pure stratospheric notes, the drama of the finale, prove beyond doubt for many people the remarkable durability of a Streisand performance which reaches its peak.

Three years later, though, Barbra herself had other views. When David Jacobs on BBC radio said to her: 'We got to love you on that record, do you particularly like it?', she replied: 'I love the song – it was an important step in my life and my career, doing that song, something that reached people, communicated; on that LP record I don't like the ending, it's much too dramatic, too big, too much discord; it's a shame. One of these days I'm going to do it over again – in my television show it was right; we changed the ending. I have to be dramatic pretty, not dramatic ugly.' Modern assessments would prove Barbra correct.

At the time, however, Columbia were nervous about the reaction to what they considered to be specialized numbers and insisted on including one popular song. Barbra chose 'A Taste of Honey', though she considered it unnecessary. Soaring sales proved her right and the album certainly didn't stand or fall on this middle-of-the-road offering, though her performance was competent enough.

All sorts of experts put forward many different reasons for

Streisand's remarkable impact on record. They ranged from the mystique which she exuded as a celebrity, her off-beat qualities, unconventional looks, forthright personality, the dramatization of her voice with its emotional content, her range, the way she attacks a song, the way she submits a song to her own being and personality, rather than the other way round. Her own views were more basic and perhaps nearer the truth. She explained later: 'People were just ready for me. Music was predominantly rock 'n' roll and there was no other major new artist around. So when I came along and did my esoteric, ethereal songs, I think people were struck by my audacity.'

Barbra certainly impressed, for this first major album won critical acclaim as well as becoming a huge financial success. Columbia's doubts vanished overnight and they quickly lined up a second album, to be called *The Second Barbra Streisand Album*. Before 1963 was out they would decide to produce a third LP, to be called *The Third Album*. As these quickly and firmly established Streisand as one of the top recording artists – at the Grammy awards her first album was announced as the best of 1963 and her 'Happy Days' won her the Best Female Vocalist category – she was thrust into a whirlwind schedule which took her on important nightclub dates, gave her lavish media attention, included key concert appearances at the Hollywood Bowl and the Coconut Grove, and took her into television studios for guest spots on America's most famous shows.

The most significant and most tantalizingly alluring appearance came on 6 October 1963 when she guested on *The Judy Garland Show* along with the Smothers Brothers and Ethel Merman. Judy's career at this time sadly had seen better days and her television variety show had been set up earlier that year as a means of repackaging the great Hollywood legend as a cosier, friendlier personality in a one-to-one setting with the viewer. Twenty-six, hour-long shows were taped, perhaps the best among them being the one which featured Streisand, though as a series they were dismally misguided and unsuccessful. Barbra's invitation to do the show came after Judy had seen a Streisand concert and, as one show-business historian put it, bringing the two greatest singers of their respective generations together was to be a milestone in television history.

The highlight of the show was also Judy's idea, a counterpoint duet with Barbra singing 'Happy Days Are Here Again' and Judy singing 'Get Happy'. These kind of set pieces can be hideously tedious, but this was an exception. In the rapport which the singers had for each other, in their vocal sensibilities and in their natural feel for a song and a lyric, and in the atmospheric presentation they were able to create visually in the studio, it was to go down as a very special experience. As Dennis M. Pallante put it, writing in *All About Barbra*: 'Everything that has been written about this duet is true. It is a classic. The two singers have such a warm rapport and obvious fondness for each other that it spills over into their singing. Both of them are in superb voice; their harmonizing is pure magic.'

Garland it seemed had been hesitant at first about getting Barbra's co-operation on the number and Dennis Pallante reports the crucial part played by the great jazz singer Mel Tormé in the scheme of things. It seems that when Tormé arrived at Judy's request early in the morning of the first day of rehearsal for the show, Judy was playing a recording of Barbra's famous version of 'Happy Days'. On his arrival Judy began the record and this time started singing 'Get Happy' in counterpoint. Tormé thought it was sensational. Taking up the story from Mel Tormé's own book *The Other Side of the Rainbow with Judy Garland on the Dawn Patrol* Pallante goes on to say that 'it was one of those rare moments when an inspired genius, in this case Judy Garland, is suddenly charged with the spark of a brilliant idea.'

But Judy was worried in case Barbra might not like the idea because 'Happy Days' was one of her signature songs. Tormé assured Judy that it was worth presenting to Barbra because after all Judy would be sacrificing one of her trademark songs for the sake of the duet.

'Later that morning,' reports Pallante, 'as Tormé was helping Streisand choose material, he suggested she sing "Happy Days". Since Barbra can sing in many different keys he chose one in his range. As he began to play and Streisand started singing, Tormé joined in with "Get Happy". Barbra loved it. She thought it was a brilliant idea, and upon learning that it was Judy's suggestion, Barbra was even further delighted.'

Another of a trilogy of major television shows in which Streisand guested in 1963 was *The Dinah Shore Show*, taped in

September and originally scheduled for December. But in the end it didn't go out until the early summer of 1964 because, it was said, it was considered the best of the bunch and was kept back so that the series could end on the highest possible note. Barbra had two featured spots and chose Streisand specials 'Cry Me a River' and 'Happy Days'. The general consensus was that she overdid the dramatics on the first number, but delivered the second with a smooth perfection well in keeping with her climbing reputation.

On *The Bob Hope Special*, Barbra once again had two solo spots in addition to a funny skit with Hope towards the end. She was projected as a major star guest raising her reputation yet again with flattering performances of 'Any Place I Hang My Hat Is Home' and 'Gotta Move'. Recalling the occasion for the Streisand special publication *All About Barbra*, Dennis M. Pallante wrote about the first number: 'It is performed with all the zest and enthusiasm this terrific singer can muster. Dressed in a long black dress, arms closely at her side, she invokes an aura of fascination. The camera slowly moves around her, capturing the free-spirited singing; and in one awkward attempt at drama, pulls back too soon toward the end of the song, leaving an almost soundless Barbra belting out the final note.

' "Gotta Move" is jazzy and sexy. Accompanied by percussive bongos, the number is exuberant and again energetic. The camera, for the most part, remains stationary, keeping Barbra in full length. No movement is needed here since it would interfere with Barbra's powerful delivery.'

The year continued at a furious pace with Barbra driving home her reputation at all levels, though her début at Las Vegas turned out to be less than satisfactory, except in a financial sense. It was July 1963 and Liberace, then at the height of his career, was responsible for Barbra adding the singular accolade of a Las Vegas engagement to her catalogue of triumphs. He had seen her at the Bon Soir and on the famous Ed Sullivan Show, and was so impressed that he wanted her as the opening act while on tour. For some reason this didn't happen, but when he went back to the Riviera Hotel at Las Vegas after a five-year absence he made sure that Barbra was booked to support him.

It was one experience in 1963 Barbra didn't much enjoy. She accused audiences of being more interested in eating and gambling than in her singing and didn't enjoy making such compromises. Brought up on a long diet of middle-of-the-road songs, presented with plenty of visual glamour, audiences found it hard to take Barbra in the Vegas environment. In appearance and in comparison with what they had become accustomed to seeing, she was dowdy and uninspiring; and to enjoy Streisand you had to pay attention and really listen. But for Barbra there were compensations in that monthly engagement. Like the $7,500-a-week fee she received; and an agreement with the management, who wanted her back whenever she chose to return.

That didn't happen for six years. More important at the time was her love and concern for Elliott Gould. While Barbra had been in Las Vegas, Elliott was opening in London in a production of *On the Town* and, as already recorded, the two spent a few idyllic days together in Britain before Streisand returned to the US to continue her whirlwind success. While in Britain Gould had intimated that he and Barbra had been married in Miami some four months before, but this wasn't so. In those early years of the 1960s the public wasn't always as prepared as now to tolerate their favourite celebrities talking about themselves living together outside marriage, and sooner than run the risk of sullying their public image Elliott resorted to the somewhat innocent deception, Barbra it seems had done the same earlier. In any event, it wasn't for long because on his return to the United States he rejoined Barbra in Los Angeles and together they flew to Lake Tahoe where Streisand had a gig lined up at Harrah's. Secretly they married at nearby Carson City, Nevada on 13 September 1963.

Making it official didn't alter anything. Their affection for each other was on the surface still as deep as ever, but it wouldn't be too long before Elliott would find Barbra's rocketing success hard to take. Already, as he returned from Britain, Barbra was commanding $5,000 a week for her show at the Coconut Grove and soon after a briefly snatched honeymoon in Las Vegas, she was being acclaimed coast-to-coast as the top young female singer in America. But for a time, Elliott was happy to thrust aside the slowly gathering disposition for him to be considered as 'Mr Streisand', and instead share fully in Barbra's triumphs which, in October, were extended significantly with the release of *The Second Barbra Streisand Album*. It had a sensational reception and by general concensus, she sounded even better than on the first album. She stamped her individuality on such long-lifers as 'Any Place I Hang My Hat Is Home', 'Lover, Come Back to Me', and added 'Too Long at the Fair' and 'My Coloring Book' from her Bon Soir/Blue Angel repertoire and 'Who Will Buy' from the stage show *Oliver*.

Public response left no one disappointed and some record shops were out of stock within twenty-four hours of receiving their initial consignment. For Barbra Streisand, it seemed, nothing could go wrong. As Rene Jordan recorded in his book *Streisand*: 'The fans turned out *en masse* for her one-night stand at the Hollywood Bowl with Sammy Davis, Jr. She went on to pack the Arie Crown Theater in Chicago for two evenings at $8,000 a performance.' There is little doubt that Streisand could have continued earning enormous sums simply by picking out the most lucrative deals which were now being dangled before her for personal appearances, record sessions, television spectaculars, guest dates – but the spirit and the emotional and creative intensity which dictated such enormous success when moving into anything new, she found difficult to sustain over long periods. Already, with a string of dates lined out ahead of her, she began to consider what else the future might hold.

Already, however, through the most complicated entanglement of circumstances involving disagreements, delays, misunderstandings, abandonments and restarts, resolve and determination, fate was taking a hand in the immediate future development of the Streisand career. The outcome was the successful presentation on Broadway of *Funny Girl*, based very loosely on the life of former *Ziegfeld* star Fanny Brice, which turned out to be a theatrical blockbuster for Streisand.

The story tells of Brice's rise to fame from the back streets of Manhattan's Lower East Side, her attempts to make her marriage to a gambler work at the cost of her career, and her subsequent return to the stage. The birth of *Funny Girl* was long and painful and more than once was in mortal danger. No show can have experienced such a precarious, perversive, emotionally draining gestation. It had been talked about seriously for three years, but it wasn't until quite late in 1963 that Barbra was linked as a possible candidate to take the Fanny Brice lead.

The show had its first public peformance in Boston on 13 January 1964 but didn't reach Broadway officially until 26 March at the Winter Garden Theater, and only then after three or four announced opening dates had been postponed and rearranged. That first performance started thirteen minutes late, but at the end the audience was ecstatic and Barbra scored an overwhelming personal triumph, taking over twenty curtain calls. *Funny Girl* was destined to run for 1,348 performances on Broadway, and then did more than 100 performances in a limited run in England at the West End's Prince of Wales Theatre.

Even in the euphoria of its instant success, the preceding many months of trauma were unlikely to have been erased from the consciousness of the few who ran the course and others who fell at numerous hurdles. For many was the time, almost until the very end, that the project looked doomed for ever.

The show that was to emerge as *Funny Girl* and become a hit on Broadway in 1964, had originated in the mind of Ray Stark, Fanny Brice's son-in-law, as a Hollywood tribute to the show-business legend. Stark, a successful press agent, had first turned to a screenplay based on Brice's career by his friend Ben Hecht, but Hollywood showed no interest. As time went on Fanny, who had been critical of Hecht's version anyway, decided to tell her own story. She had completed the autobiography which was in the hands of a publisher when she died at the age of fifty-nine. That was in 1951, but Stark still hankered after the story as a movie. So he blocked publication, buying the printing plates from the publisher for a reputed $50,000. Still he had no luck in convincing a major studio to take the Fanny Brice story.

By 1960 Stark had become a successful film producer and had tried repeatedly though unsuccessfully to develop a suitable screenplay that would interest Hollywood. Determined to see the project through, he turned to screenwriter Isobel Lennart's more endearing version of his late mother-in-law's life which she had written under the title of *My Man*. Still unable to raise any interest in Hollywood, he reluctantly turned to Broadway, intending to present *My Man* as a play.

Two crucial developments now occurred. Stark formed a partnership with David Merrick, a producer of stage musicals and one of the most powerful men in show business at that time, and it was Merrick who convinced Stark that *My Man* should be produced as a musical. Secondly, composer Jule Styne, already a prolific, respected and highly successful

Broadway and Hollywood writer, was called in along with Stephen Sondheim to produce the score, following their successful collaboration on *Gypsy*. Isobel Lennart reworked her script and Styne and Sondheim got ready to produce the music and the lyrics.

Meanwhile Stark had sent a copy of the script to Mary Martin, then a major star. Merrick and Stark were delighted to hear that she was interested, but lyricist Sondheim took a different view, complaining that she would be wrong for the part. Fanny Brice was, of course, Jewish and Sondheim insisted that only a Jewish girl – and a Jewish-looking girl at that – would be right for the part. He left on this point of principle, but thankfully for the project, Styne stayed, bringing in Bob Merrill as Sondheim's replacement after a tedious three-month delay. Work restarted but as time went on Mary Martin lost interest and the show was put in doubt again.

By this time Styne and Merrill had worked up what must rate as one of the greatest scores of all time. It included 'People', 'Don't Rain On My Parade' and 'I'm the Greatest Star'. Though not considered a singer, Anne Bancroft was approached and was interested until she heard the songs. She knew her limitations as a singer and turned the offer down. Carol Burnett and Eydie Gorme were then considered, but Burnett shared Sondheim's view. Gorme might have had the ability musically, but would only be interested if husband singer Steve Lawrence could co-star as gambler Nick Arnstein, the ill-fated lover in Fanny's life. Perhaps few would deny that Lawrence would have performed better as Arnstein than Sydney Chaplin, who eventually would be cast in the role, but as a combination the famous musical partnership wasn't seriously considered for the show. And according to a much later analysis of the situation by distinguished Streisand enthusiast Allison J. Waldman, it is perhaps just as well. For according to Waldman '... while Steve Lawrence may have been a good Nick, Eydie Gorme would probably not have been a good Fanny. She needs to be the stronger half of the duo. Gorme has always played the weaker half opposite Lawrence ...'. In the same appraisal, in the publication *All About Barbra*, Waldman assesses Lawrence. 'He would have been a terrific choice to play Nick Arnstein.'

Shirley MacLaine was another candidate, among others, but it was left to producer David Merrick, almost in desperation, to

think of Streisand. The choice had the backing of Jule Styne and
of Garson Kanin, who had come in for Bob Fosse when the latter
withdrew from the project. But casting problems persisted.
Fanny Brice's daughter Fran objected to Streisand portraying
her mother. She said she was too sloppy and not special like her
mother, while Fanny's later husband Billy Rose, in a magazine
article, claimed that there wasn't an actress around who could
portray Fanny Brice with any conviction.

Despite these protestations Styne, Merrick and Kanin
persisted in their choice of Streisand and opened negotiations,
though Ray Stark was even then against the choice. Nor was
Barbra at this stage overjoyed at the prospect. Having to
submerge her own character into somebody else's life didn't
instantly appeal and the duality of her personality, which had
been manifest over recent times, was once again evident: she
doubted her ability to do it. Reading the script made her mind
up and a particularly good deal worked out by her four-man
team of shrewd negotiators led by her personal manager Marty
Erlichman, put it beyond doubt.

It is astonishing now to contemplate how anyone other than
Streisand could have been considered for the Fanny Brice role.
The two had so much in common that Barbra stands out
overwhelmingly as the obvious choice. Their ethnic back-
grounds matched. Both had spent their early days in Brooklyn
dreaming of a future as a star on Broadway. Neither was a
traditional beauty.

So with that crucial casting completed, the way was surely
now clear to move swiftly to get the show on the road. Yet new
problems arose, one serious enough to put the project in
jeopardy. Ray Stark and David Merrick disagreed on some point
and the latter stormed off. But the issue which now emerged to
put everyone concerned into an advanced state of apoplexy was
Streisand's contact, which it was now realized had been signed
by Merrick. Stark must have thought that Streisand was a
gremlin, put there by some kind of divine intervention to
sabotage the show. For here he was, having overcome his
doubts about Barbra being right for the role, now without his
leading lady while Merrick held Streisand's contract, but didn't
have a show. It had been done this way quite sensibly to avoid
having to place the two-weeks' salary bond insisted upon by the
Actors' Equity which would guarantee a severance pay-out for

the cast should the show be a flop. Merrick, an established producer of substance, was not required to place such a bond. Stark, on the other hand, would have been under such an obligation since he had not previously put on a Broadway show. That is why Merrick had signed the original contract.

For a week or so the show looked as if it were falling apart. Stark was furious and on the brink of pulling out. Streisand's agents spied the chink of a chance to get an even better deal for their client. There was no chance of Merrick returning. It appears that Garson Kanin, who, if lacking some of the natural flair of Bob Fosse whom he had replaced as director, was now called upon to use his skills of diplomacy and negotiation if *Funny Girl* was to be saved. He arbitrated and appeased and in the end Stark did yeoman service in being able to negotiate a new contract with Barbra. With the backing of Kanin and Styne, Streisand was not only to secure the role once again, but her negotiators were able to finalize a better financial deal.

Having Streisand once more on the project, now considered the key element to any success the show might achieve, progress was renewed, but the going wasn't easy even now. Kanin didn't want Sydney Chaplin in the role of Nick Arnstein, but lost out probably because Barbra didn't seem to have an opinion one way or the other. Conflicting temperaments among those running the show seemed to put everything on a short fuse and Kanin had to work hard once more on Stark who, after seeing Streisand's early rehearsal work, voiced disappointments and doubts. Even before these cleared up, second thoughts were being expressed about Chaplin. Brought in largely perhaps to appease an insistent Frances Stark, Fanny Brice's daughter, who saw mileage in having the son of the great Chaplin in the top billing (probably correctly too), Chaplin didn't consider himself a singer. Nor did many others and Chaplin saw his role being emasculated as songs had to be changed and cut and the script rewritten. Not surprisingly he got tetchy and threatened to quit. By this time Streisand wouldn't have shed a tear at the prospect because they weren't getting on at all well. Legend has it that the ending of the show was rewritten more than forty times before *Funny Girl* played on Broadway for the first time.

Despite all the problems, the show was put on before a paying audience for the first time on 13 January 1964, in Boston at the start of its preliminary out-of-town run. Extreme weather conditions delayed the curtain-raising, but the show overran by at least an hour anyway and the audience didn't get away until about 1.45 a.m. Reviews were poor and the cast was thrown into despair. There were panic changes to costumes and new sets were brought in to ensure balance and continuity as whole sections were discarded.

Incredulous as it seems now, a near-victim of the purge was the Jule Styne/Bob Merrill number 'People'. Two eccentric circumstances saved this number, which was to become an enormous gross earner for Streisand, from being butchered. It happened after the company had moved on to the Forest Theater in Philadelphia on 4 February 1964, for a further three weeks of trial runs.

Cast morale was low and the mania for change continued. Taking an hour off a show inevitably means some savage cutting and just before the Philadelphia opening Kanin moved to delete 'People'. Never it seems a particular favourite of Streisand's, Kanin ran into unexpected opposition from Bob Merrill, who proclaimed its greatness, staking the song's future on the audience's reaction at the opening performance. The other stroke of fortune was that Barbra had earlier recorded the song and it had become an outstanding hit with the record-buying public. During the performance it stopped the show and earned an encore. It was also warmly applauded during the overture.

Funny Girl had gone through a metamorphosis since the early concept of the show. Doubts about the script, presentation, the score, Chaplin's attitude as he saw his part being reworked and played down in the interest of saving running time and other factors, all this had combined with the in-fighting which had gone on among those engaged in putting on the show to strengthen the one stable element in the whole sorry situation: the character of Fanny Brice as portrayed by Barbra Streisand. She was given additional numbers and featured more prominently in certain scenes. Her always pivotal role had now become a sheet anchor. Abetted by a script which had moved away from a close portrayal of Brice, vesting more responsibility for its success on Streisand's own talent, personality and charisma, it was seen clearly at Philadelphia that *Funny Girl's* success or failure was very much down to Streisand.

The off-stage blood-letting, however, hadn't quite finished. As the spectre of that Broadway opening loomed, Ray Stark was still looking for changes and Garson Kanin, wearied from the prolonged toil of buoying up *Funny Girl* over many months, ended his period as director, though retained a financial interest in the show. Jerome Robbins, whom Stark had seriously considered as director at the start of rehearsals following his *West Side Story* success, was brought in to contribute fresh ideas and tighten up production. He certainly made an impact, for less than an hour before curtain-up on opening night at the Winter Garden on Broadway, he had the cast on stage rehearsing a new version of the final scene.

The critics were generous and rightly so because, however you looked at it, *Funny Girl* was good entertainment; although reviews exposed the weak areas with brutal clarity. The second act was censured for losing its way, Sydney Chaplin's Nick Arnstein was at best tepidly dismissed, perhaps escaping stronger rebuke amid the excitement of a spectacular first night; and the opportunity to recapture the spectacle and glamour of the famous *Ziegfeld Follies* was never firmly grasped. But, as the critics were willing to concede, the compensations were ample. First, Jule Styne's score was exceptional, rich in melodic scale and popular potential, and gloriously enhanced by Streisand's technique and interpretation.

For the remainder, it was Barbra Streisand all the way. The critics raved over her performance. During those long traumatic months of rehearsal, notwithstanding the tensions, arguments, script butcherings and repeated rewrites, Barbra had absorbed much of the character of Fanny Brice. But, as Allison J. Waldman was later to point out: 'As the creators and Barbra admitted after the opening, *Funny Girl* was not a perfectly accurate biography of Fanny Brice. They decided instead to capture the essence of the girl/woman Fanny was, during the period of the show. Barbra felt Fanny was as close to her as if they were sisters.' That obviously added conviction to the portrayal, which that first-night audience, at a subliminal level, might well have sensed. But at a conscious level they were rooting for Barbra Streisand, no one else. It was the moment she became 'a star'.

Barbra was now thrust into the media world of the megastar. She was high-profiled in *Time* and *Life* in consecutive months and was in demand for interviews, pictures, comments and quotes. The idolatry stretched beyond Broadway. Her two albums had given her an international reputation, now being bolstered with each new performance of *Funny Girl*. Her star status affected every aspect of her life. Husband Elliott Gould, struggling with only marginal success to make his own way to the top, battled to keep in touch with his wife, to retain meaning and relevance within a Streisand lifestyle which she now found hard to control.

She was the property of the nation as the Streisand look became the latest cult. The make-up, hairstyle, clothes – all the features for which she had been ridiculed or ignored in the past – suddenly meant everything. She had soared to fame in the part of Fanny Brice. But it was Barbra Streisand everyone wanted to know about, to see, to picture, to mimic. Nobody doubted Streisand's gigantic talent before *Funny Girl*, but some commentators picked on elegance as the one quality until then absent from Barbra's personality. It was *Funny Girl* which gave her elegance and to prove the point she appeared modelling clothes in the pages of the influential *Vogue* three times during 1964. She led the day as a trendsetter, celebrated within the lofty echelons of the 'best dressed' listings.

But the sudden change dug deep into Barbra's own psyche, bringing doubts and fears. Any remnant of privacy was gone and the stampede for autographs whenever she was spotted could be a physical hazard. She found the adulation hard to live with because '… Everything you do can destroy the image,' she explained. Not that Barbra was ungrateful, though being ungrateful, or grateful for that matter, are sentiments not strongly evident in the Streisand make-up. She had worked hard, sacrificed herself for her art and sure, she deserved the adulation and wanted it. But the real excitement, she revealed at the time, was in the hope, in striving for something and not really in achieving it. Thus, Streisand found the routine of a long-running show hard to live with and long before the two-year run on Broadway was ended, she was privately irritated, impatient and artistically unfulfilled.

But if *Funny Girl*, notwithstanding its continued success, fell short of her needs, there were other declarations of her dazzling status as an entertainer which, even if they exposed the fallibility of her talent, at least took her mind off what she was later to describe as like being locked up in prison.

The release of her *Third Album* had been timed for the opening of *Funny Girl* and while musically disappointing some of her followers, it quickly was to establish its own special place among the growing number of younger and perhaps less discerning fans. She detached herself from the agony of less complimentary reviews, finding consolation in the truth that she had been criticized earlier for being predictable and turning every song into a Streisand special, yet couldn't please now that she had deliberately set out to be different.

If perhaps a cynical response, the Tony awards in May 1964, diverted her mind. She ran close to honours, but although *Funny Girl* received eight nominations, Barbra lost out at a personal level to Carol Channing for her role in *Hello Dolly!*

A month later Barbra, through a company she had formed with Elliott Gould, signed with CBS for her to do three television specials over the next two years for a guaranteed $1 million. The fight for Streisand's signature on the contract had been so intense that she had been given all the freedom and scope she needed to put on the kind of show she wanted. Moreover, it was to lead to an unprecedented $5 million contract from CBS for a series of television spectaculars over the next ten years. In July she was paid $80,000 for a Sunday-night concert at the Forest Hills stadium where 15,000 fans screamed their undivided loyalty.

Nine months later Streisand taped her first television special for CBS. First put out on 28 April 1965 under the title *My Name Is Barbra*, it was another enormous triumph. Its success was to be consolidated later when released as a double album. Back on the daily routine of *Funny Girl*, the relationship between Streisand and her leading man, never blissful, had not improved over the months. Whatever the reasons, Chaplin was now determined to leave the show, despite his run-of-play contract. In mid-June 1965 his role of Nick Arnstein was taken over by understudy George Reeder, prior to Johnny Desmond moving into the show in August. In September television honoured *My Name Is Barbra* with five Emmy awards, one not unexpectedly being in recognition of Barbra's outstanding personal contribution. Her second television spectacular, *Color Me Barbra*, was another outstanding success. It was screened in March 1966, just a couple of weeks before her much-ballyhooed opening with *Funny Girl* in Britain.

London and the United Kingdom, much as New York and the USA, capitulated to the Streisand magic. Now reputed to be the highest-paid singer in the world, the thought of appearing in Britain none the less made her nervous. The media hype which had preceded her across the Atlantic would need to be justified, but that didn't scare Streisand. Typically, it was whether she could conquer her passionate need to create Fanny Brice once again in her own image which was the real challenge. Sustaining the legend was another matter.

The opening of *Funny Girl* in London took place on Wednesday, 13 April 1966. Five days before, Sophia Loren had shocked the film world by marrying Carlo Ponti in France while he was still legally married in Italian law, and five days later *The Sound of Music* captured the year's Oscar for the best film. By midnight, both events had been pushed to one side by the dramatic success of Streisand's début in London. Herbert Kretzmer in the *Daily Express* wrote that Barbra lived up to the legend. 'The girl and the myth are indivisible,' he reported. The *Sunday Telegraph* described her as a 'prodigious and unique creature', and although some of the upmarket titles maintained their self-appointed reputation for containing their enthusiasm and excitement under the guise of maturity and experience, there were enough reports to give a glow to the West End run. 'A star is a girl who can hush a thousand people into silence and a second later make them explode with joy. By these tests and any other you can think of, Barbra Streisand is a star, and *Funny Girl*, which had its official opening after the biggest build-up since D-Day, is her show,' ran one review.

The opening was a glittering occasion endowed with the ultimate accolade of a royal presence. Princess Margaret was there with the Earl of Snowdon and afterwards Barbra was introduced to the Princess, who told her she had all her records. It is hard to know how Barbra felt on such an occasion. She was always her own person, gripped by self-doubts and often instinctively defensive in unsure situations. She said later: 'I didn't know what to say, so I just stood there and replied "Yeah"?'

On the whole though, and despite the success of *Funny Girl* in London, where advance bookings set box-office records, the run was not renowned for its back-stage harmony. There were numerous discordant occasions and Streisand was accused of being difficult and hard to work with. She didn't mix with other members of the cast yet, it was alleged, was quick enough to send critical notes to those she felt ought to be doing more towards the success of the show. Her co-star Michael Craig publicly came to her defence when she was unjustly accused of not inviting members of the cast to an opening-night party, but Barbra did privately admit to Michael during rehearsals that *Funny Girl* wasn't fun for her any more.

Soon after the London opening Barbra and Elliott announced that she was pregnant, but, although she carried out her full commitment to the West End show, there were carping accusations that she was being tempted back to the US by the prospect of higher-paid engagements there. It is true that she did honour a number of previously booked highly lucrative engagements on her return to the United States, but these were one-nighters and considerably less physically exhausting and stressful than her commitment to *Funny Girl* had been. In London she was required to produce a highly charged performance eight times a week – every week – literally carrying the responsibility of a show which depended in total on her being there. Admired and loved as a performer, Streisand wasn't the most liked person in London. The few performances she missed because of her pregnancy, but before it was publicly announced, were put down to temperament and her fading interest in *Funny Girl*, while her insistence on leaving the sell-out show at the end of the fourteen-week engagement disappointed many people.

The money-grabbing allegations which a tactless Streisand had to endure in London could be seen in a more balanced light on her return to the United States, where her pregnancy forced her to pull out of sixteen of a scheduled sell-out twenty-city tour on medical advice. And, although she had done nothing to conceal her monetary worth as the highest-paid entertainer in the world, she had sacrificed many thousands of dollars – possibly more – by agreeing to the limited London engagement.

For the moment, however, having a baby meant more than singing, acting, performing, making money, and at 3 p.m. on 29 December 1966, at Mount Sinai hospital in New York, Barbra and Elliott's son was born, to be called Jason Emanuel, the second name in memory of Barbra's beloved father she had never known.

5 To Hollywood on a Multi-million Dollar Début

Ray Stark's vision of committing the Fanny Brice story to film may have gained considerable strength from the Broadway and West End successes of *Funny Girl*, but Hollywood history provided little ground for optimism. In 1939 the 20th Century Fox production, *Rose of Washington Square*, with Alice Faye in the role of Brice, had run into all kinds of problems. The story line had wandered significantly from the facts of Fanny Brice's life and both she and Nicky Arnstein had sued the film company. A nasty situation ended with out-of-court settlements for undisclosed sums. Nor was the film encouraging commercially, for, despite the presence of Faye, who had risen to fame on the success of crusading musicals like *On the Avenue*, *In Old Chicago* and *Alexander's Ragtime Band*, and the new Hollywood heart-throb sensation, Tyrone Power, it fell well short of being a major box-office hit.

Yet twenty-five years later, Stark was determined that *Funny Girl* would become a successful movie. To bolster his confidence he now could draw on the enormous success of *Funny Girl* on Broadway and in the West End. He was certain he could now make his stage triumph a blockbuster on screen. The key element in the equation was Streisand, a key element he had already secured. For with opportunism and foresight he had persuaded Barbra to sign a multi-picture deal with him while she was still busy doing the show on Broadway. At first she had resisted, not wanting to commit herself so comprehensively, but Stark was shrewd enough to know that one vital circumstance gave him what he believed to be an overpowering advantage: Barbra's driving ambition to become a movie star.

Even after her phenomenal impact on stage, in the recording studio, on personal appearances and in front of the television camera, she wanted more than anything in the world to fulfil her childhood ambition from her Brooklyn days nurtured in the gloom of Loew's Kings Theater on Flatbush Avenue and become a film star. For Barbra, being a star had always meant being a film star. That ambition transcended everything. She agreed to Ray Stark's conditions and signed a contract.

Such indeed was the enormity of her standing as a high-profile entertainer that when she set out for Hollywood at the start of her cinema career, she had signed to do in all six movies at earnings moderately estimated to be well into the multi-million dollar bracket. It was unprecedented in the long history of Hollywood, for at this point Barbra Streisand, despite her reputation in the theatre, through nightclub engagements, on record and in television, was untried and inexperienced in the movie business. Who could guarantee that she wouldn't be like Fanny Brice herself, who achieved enormous stardom on the live stage but never made it in pictures? But Ray Stark and others were eager to take the risk. For *Funny Girl* her basic salary would be $200,000, for *On a Clear Day You Can See Forever*, a picture already scheduled, $350,000. In addition to her commitments to Stark for four pictures in all, she had also signed with 20th Century Fox for the starring role in the film version of *Hello Dolly!* at a guaranteed $750,000, plus a percentage of the take.

If the intoxication of motherhood for a while diminished the feverish urge for Barbra to extend her professional career following the birth of Jason, by the time she arrived in Los Angeles in May 1967 she was ready for Hollywood; and Hollywood was certainly ready for Streisand. The iniquitous studio star system which had none the less galvanized the film industry during the Second World War and immediately after, had long since disappeared and in its wake financial pressures, studio buy-outs and amalgamations had spawned more commercial attitudes and cut traditions.

In the new order run by accountants and administrators, brought about by the threat to big-screen movie making by television, the coming of a brand-new superstar of the magnitude and extravagant talent of Streisand was in itself a major happening and Barbra's arrival on the scene was in the very best traditions of fabled Hollywood. When she stepped off the plane, as James Spada has reported 'She was accompanied by her husband, her baby, her dog, a half dozen trunks, and reams of newspaper copy.' The dog, christened Sadie, was a white poodle presented to her by the cast of the Broadway presentation of *Funny Girl*.

Elliott Gould's sojourn in Hollywood was fleeting since he had been successful in securing a part in the Broadway production of *Little Murders*. Barbra based herself in a rented house once the home of none other than Greta Garbo and shaped up defiantly to a Hollywood press corps psyched for battle. For a start, reports that Streisand was likely to make $1 million out of the forthcoming movie was considered excessive even by Hollywood's extravagant standards, and for someone who hadn't yet made a movie, almost obscene. The hostile reaction also fed off the poor reviews given to Barbra's third television special, *The Belle of Fourteenth Street*. These surfaced at the time of her arrival in Hollywood, as inconveniently as the critical reviews were unexpected. Some useful copy was also anticipated in the selection of the legendary William Wyler to direct the film. A Hollywood giant of resolute views and with the reputation of making sure he got his own way with the stars who worked with him, Wyler, a supreme Hollywood craftsman renowned for award-winning dramas like *Wuthering Heights* and *The Little Foxes*, was expected to have anything but a sympathetic, understanding, if professional relationship with the equally dogmatic, individualistic Streisand.

Wyler, despite his gigantic reputation in Hollywood, also had never made a musical and although some of the songs from the stage version of *Funny Girl* were eventually to be cut, the film's success would still rest on its impact as a musical vehicle. Critics of these cuts would later suggest that they were made as much because of Wyler's lack of vision and experience in working on a film musical as they were by the contingencies of a different medium.

The choice of Omar Sharif in the role of Nicky Arnstein was also curious and despite his professional performance his obvious Middle-Eastern accent rankled with some critics. But at a more popular level his casting, after a number of more established Hollywood stars including Frank Sinatra had reportedly been approached, was sound. For in 1962 Sharif had scored an enormous success as the newest international heart-throb in David Lean's epic, *Lawrence of Arabia*, for which he won an Oscar nomination. So there was little doubt that *Funny Girl* would benefit in box-office takings from his presence.

Like the stage show, the Hollywood version of *Funny Girl* went through numerous rewrites. Credited with the screenplay in the final titles was Isobel Lennart, who had worked closely with Barbra on the stage presentation. It is to her credit as a person and her resilience as a screen-writer that she withstood what must have been enormous pressure from many sides, producing in the end a version of the story which not only she could be happy with, but which triumphed with the public and satisfied most of her colleagues on the set. For some diehards it was bound to rate second best to the stage version, the so-called over-dramatization of what was in essense a simple tale, being strongly contested. But only Jule Styne perhaps raised a dissenting voice about the film itself and that only with the very ending, claiming that in her final singing of 'My Man' Brice's character changed and she was presented as self-pitying and timid, which she never was; though this could have been as much a criticism of Wyler or Streisand as of Lennart. But Styne did say later that *Funny Girl* was the best movie that had ever been made of one of his stage musicals.

The screen version of *Funny Girl* confirmed Barbra's feelings that making movies was what she really wanted to do. The medium satisfied her obsession with perfection, at the same time cutting out the need for tedious repeat performances. Once she had a scene as good as it could be made, the camera was able to record it and it was there for ever. By comparison, going through the same routine twice nightly on stage was a drudge. She was to demonstrate this predilection by starring in no fewer than nine films during the 1970s.

In *Funny Girl* Barbra grabbed the chance to recreate her famous role on film. She relished being in front of the cameras, her personality, style, sensitivity even, jumping out from the screen in a vivid and realistic example of her newly discovered art. As one critic said afterwards: 'All a show needs is Barbra Streisand.' She instinctively seemed at home on film, her performance so much in a class of its own that one self-confessed fan was driven to claim that 'They certainly broke the mould after Streisand.' Others would quickly agree that Streisand is a genuinely unique performer and if in *Funny Girl* her rapid-fire dialogue and level of enthusiasm is very occasionally just a fraction hard to live with, these are minute prices to pay for such a sparkling individual performance.

From the softly haunting theme of 'People' coming through the opening credits to the powerfully dramatic finale when Barbra in close-up and wearing a stunningly simple black dress against a dark background sings 'My Man', haltingly at first as she fights back the tears, but with such emotion and feeling, Streisand underwrites her natural fusion with the cinema screen as she comprehensively submits her whole being to the audience. She seemed instantly at home with the more intimate medium of film, her nuances and subtlety of performance gaining immeasurably from the closer scrutiny the camera exacts. She was even better on film than on a theatrical stage, the intimacy of the cinema, as writer Allison J. Waldman later observed, '... bringing out the detail and texture of the performance. In *Funny Girl*, all the vulnerability, energy and honesty Barbra imbued in Fanny, jumped off the screen. After years of believing that Barbra was an ugly duckling, the camera revealed her to be a swan.'

This was in itself a surprising and remarkable aspect of Streisand in *Funny Girl*. On film she still lacks the features of a classic beauty. Her eyes are too narrow, her nose too long and her mouth too wide, but somehow she carries more sensual and volatile attraction in one modest movement, one searching gaze, even a self-conscious giggle, than many an established screen siren during the length of an entire movie. She is at the same time precocious, vulnerable and provocative. 'Barbra was believable as Fanny the singer, Fanny the comedienne, Fanny the girl, and (especially) Fanny the lover,' wrote Allison J. Waldman. 'The sexual tension vital to Fanny and Nick's love affair would not have been present in the film if Barbra Streisand had failed to possess this special ingredient, this very personal sexual subtlety.'

Contributing significantly to Streisand's visual screen persona was the gifted Harry Stradling, a cinematographer of great distinction who worked closely with Barbra to achieve those vital, closely defined personal images. His skill and sensitivity

enabled him to light her unusual features to emphasize her
translucent beauty and her flawless skin, and his work on *Funny
Girl* was justly acknowledged with an Oscar nomination. Barbra
was so impressed with his work that she insisted on him being
brought in on *Hello Dolly!*, yet again on *On a Clear Day You Can
See Forever*, and they were together once more on her fourth
film, *The Owl and the Pussycat*. Sadly, half-way through the
shooting of the picture he died from a heart attack. They had a
special rapport and Stradling admired Barbra immensely. He
once told writer Dennis M. Pallante: 'She is one of the greatest
talents I have ever worked with. She knows what's good and
what's not good, what height the camera should be and just
where it should be placed for her close-ups. The contours of her
face give her a rare beauty.'

The film, a Willie Wyler–Ray Stark production presented by
Columbia Pictures and Stark's own company, Rastar Productions, follows the early career of Fanny Brice and is told in
flash-back. As many home-video fans will testify, it survives the
intervening twenty-three years with distinction. The film por-
trays a vintage Streisand playing herself as much as Fanny Brice
while displaying all her outstanding talent as a singer, sensitive
actress and an exceptionally fine and sophisticated comedienne.
In two specific ways the picture breaks new ground. A
courageous opening shows a rear view of Streisand against the
neon-lighted exterior of the new Amsterdam Theater on
Broadway with the Fanny Brice name proclaimed as the star of
the *Ziegfeld Follies*, but with the background playing of 'People'
fading. She crosses the road and walks reflectively into the
empty theatre, hesitating here, searching deep into her thoughts
here. *Still there is no background music*, the only sound being her
footsteps. This arresting opening, a bold film gesture at the time,
is punctuated first by Fanny as she looks into the mirror and
murmurs to herself 'Hello gorgeous' – a phrase later remembered
by Streisand to the delight of a star-studded Hollywood audience
and repeated as she turned to look at the Oscar which had just
been presented to her at the 1968 awards ceremony; then by
Streisand again as she fingers a bar or two of 'People' on the
stage piano. This magical opening, extending through almost
four minutes of film time, peaks dramatically when Barbra
wanders to centre stage and with the camera angle from behind
her picking up an empty auditorium, her mind is suddenly filled

with the swelling applause of a full house greeting their star, which she mockingly silences with a machine-gun simulation, sweeping first the stalls and then the upper seats.

The other special significance of the picture is when, on two brief occasions, the action is frozen as Fanny's reactions to the situations are conveyed in Streisand's voice-over asides. The narrative deployment of this technique was adapted and used repeatedly and effectively years later by Streisand as a special feature in conveying the thoughts and reactions of Yentl when making the picture which had been her burning ambition for fifteen years.

Funny Girl became a spectacular screen début for Barbra Streisand. She gave a compelling performance and seemed made for movies, completely relaxed and able to respond with a beguiling relish to a demanding medium until then unfamiliar to her. The picture has the present dissolving into memories of the past as Fanny sits in an aisle seat in the third row of the stalls before her nightly performance. She is a big star and the film recalls how it all began – from her audacious and hilarious début at Keeney's Music Hall in a roller-skating routine when she can't even skate, her antics bringing the house down so that she is quickly pushed back on stage for an impromptu solo encore in which she sings 'I'd rather be blue, thinking of you' – to her first meeting with the great impresario Florenz Ziegfeld, played by the redoubtable Walter Pidgeon, and the captivating lover and husband-to-be Nicky Arnstein (Omar Sharif). Both encounters individually were significant, character fundamentals of Brice, and Streisand even more so, being revealed in two particular sequences. The first points up Streisand's uncompromising stance when she feels strongly to be right; the second, the implicit right she exercises as an actress and singer to have a say in the material she should perform and in the development of her career.

In the first she has just been taken on by Ziegfeld and the great man has put her in a lavish production number based on seasonal brides in which she is to sing 'His love makes me beautiful'. It is lavish, flowing, colourful, lilting and serious with gorgeous long-limbed showgirls on stage in extravagant costumes, Barbra emerging demure and prim in a stunning 'white-and-pure' bridal gown. But before the show she is unhappy with the words she is required to say about herself being beautiful and attractive and complains to the mighty Ziegfeld that coming from her they won't sound right or convincing. Merely questioning the man makes everyone within ear-shot wince, so powerful a figure is Ziegfeld, but Barbra is unmoved. He insists that she performs it as he has dictated and summarily ignores her when she defiantly calls after his departing figure: 'You win – you don't win fair, but you win.'

You can't help but fear for Brice's future when Streisand appears in the scene before a paying audience as, shock and horror, a very pregnant young bride with a pillow stuffed up her front and hamming the part for all it's worth. Stage-hands are left open-mouthed and Ziegfeld is outraged, but after a moment of incredulity the audience loves it and acclaims Barbra's performance with a reception more resounding than ever it would have received if played straight as Ziegfeld had intended. In her dressing room afterwards Streisand says how sorry she is to have defied Ziegfeld, explaining again that she couldn't play it straight, it wouldn't have been right for her, adding that this way '... they laughed with me, not at me.' She demonstrates her handling of an audience with the explanation: 'It was my joke. I wanted them to laugh.'

Ziegfeld tells her later to add a certain song to her act but, though inexperienced and so much in awe of the legendary showman, she still finds the courage to stick by her principles, claiming that she must choose the songs she sings – a Streisand characteristic if ever there was one.

The picture traces the newly scripted version of the Fanny Brice–Nicky Arnstein story, the development of their tempestuous affair; their ill-fated marriage ·and the birth of their daughter; the soaring success of Fanny's career to the top as Flo Ziegfeld's greatest star; Nick's famous success and eventual demise as a professional gambler and, owing a fortune as his luck with the cards fails him, his self-confessed implication in a phoney bond embezzlement deal and a two-year gaol sentence. Fanny has been too wrapped up in her own glittering success to notice Nick's plight and when she does, shocked and repentant, her well-intentioned plans to help only add to his resentment.

She persuades one of Nick's contacts to offer him a partnership in a new gambling club, supposedly requiring no up-front investment and bringing him a cut of the profits for running the place. Nick can't believe it's true – nobody, not even a long-standing contact, can offer a deal that generous. Then he gradually realizes what has happened and is stunned as Fanny admits it was all her idea and that she had privately agreed to put up Nick's $50,000 stake on condition that her involvement be kept a secret. Nick is angry and embittered. He feels humiliated but Fanny, desperately striving to preserve their love for each other and their marriage, pleads: 'I was just trying to help. When I saw how unhappy you were I had to do something …'.

But it is all too late. The love they shared had been unable to bridge the gap as her career soars to the dizziest of heights as Ziegfeld's greatest star while his gambling luck runs out, plunging him deeply in debt. His inability to live in Fanny's shadow catches up with him and he says he wants her to divorce him. Sadly he tells her: 'We are just not good for each other. There is no way I can catch up with you.' But she persuades him to delay things until he has finished his prison sentence (eighteen months with remission), but as Nick turns and walks away he calls back prophetically: 'So long … Funny Girl.'

It is here that the flash-back ends. After Nick's departure the saddened Fanny moves gently, plaintively into a superb interpretation of the title song with Barbra at her most exquisite as this beautiful song ends with us back in the present with Fanny in her third-row seat in the stalls of the New Amsterdam Theater. It is eighteen months on and as Flo Ziegfeld comes into her dressing room before the opening of the show, she tells him, looking forward to Nick's freedom: 'I don't know if Nick wants to go on' – but if he does she tells Ziegfeld that she won't make the same mistakes and '… it might mean giving up the theatre.'

Applying her make-up, she looks up and sees Nick there, reflected in the mirror. She turns, filled with emotion. It is a poignant scene as they slowly and gently embrace, but however she may seem to desire their reconciliation, there can only really be one outcome. Sympathetically, he tells her: 'Fanny, I've had eighteen months to think about us … it's over.' The call boy breaks into this tenderest of scenes with Miss Brice's fifteen- and then five-minute calls, then 'Goodbye Fanny,' and, as the door closes and Nick has gone, a tearful 'Goodbye Nick.' Fanny walks on stage choked with emotion and fighting hard to control her tears, she begins haltingly '… Oh my man I love him so …' – the opening line of an outstanding and emotionally charged fade-out of 'My Man' to bring the film to an end.

The picture has many choice moments, a lilting and exhilarating score by Jule Styne and Bob Merrill, and despite the comments of Thomas G. Aylesworth who, in his *History of Movie Musicals*, singles it out as an example of 'great film makers (Wyler in this instance) who have tried musicals and not quite captured the magic', is rated highly as a musical by many observers. Few would deny, however, that the picture was overshadowed by the quality and dynamism of Streisand's personal performance. The same writer claims a much wider concensus with this broader assessment of Barbra: 'As Fanny, Barbra Streisand made her film début and won the Academy Award as best actress for her trouble. She was simply fabulous – brassy and vulnerable – and was able to toss off such lines as (indicating her nose): "You think beautiful girls are going to stay in style forever?" And what she did with the Robert Merrill–Jule Styne songs like "People" and "Don't Rain on My Parade" was perfection.'

The latter had been the *tour de force* of the stage presentation, saved as a rousing finale, and indeed retained that distinction in the picture though brought in earlier as Fanny hitches a lift on a New York tug-boat to catch up with Nick, who is on his way to Europe. The former, arguably Streisand's most popular song of all time though reportedly never one of her personal favourites, comes in the scene where she received her first screen kiss. She and Nick have only recently met and after celebrating Fanny's breakthrough success with *Ziegfeld* at a party with her family and friends at her mother's saloon in Henry Street, she is in the deserted street outside saying goodnight to Nick. Her portrayal of the youthful, innocent Fanny is excellent, her dependence on snap-response humour to distance herself from emotional advances she doesn't quite know how to handle being particularly finely drawn. For instance, after she has captivated him with a beautifully restrained version of 'People' there is silence as he walks towards her. 'Fanny, you're an enchanting girl,' he says, obviously much attracted. 'I wish I could get to know you better.'

'So give me six good reasons why not,' she responds impudently, taking the emotional sting out of the situation. 'Just one,' he says, 'I have to catch a train for Kentucky early in the morning.'

'What's in Kentucky?' queries Barbra. 'Oh, a half interest in a little farm. I breed horses,' he responds. Disarmingly Barbra counters; 'What's the matter, they can't do it alone?' She then walks him to his car, parked a few yards away. He says: 'You know if you weren't in a show I think I'd have asked you to come with me. Too bad isn't it?' Again, not sure how to handle the situation, Fanny resorts to humour: 'I don't know,' she says, 'what with the *Follies* and an indecent proposal it's been quite a night – it was indecent, wasn't it?' conveyed with that singularly Streisand look which suggests that, theoretically at least, she'd be disappointed if it hadn't been. 'Very,' he says. Barbra again: 'Thank God, at least I can tell Mrs Strakosh that things are looking up.' It's a tender moment and Barbra's first screen kiss follows – soft and gentle lasting a moderate three seconds. Then Nick gets into his car and drives away. Alone, Barbra balances along the curb edge on her way back into the saloon, her arms stretched out at shoulder length like a trapeze artist. Background music eases into the scene, Barbra starts humming the tune, then the music and the voice open up into a magnificent few bars of 'People' to end a sensitive and excellent sequence.

Barbra handles the scene with a joyous delicacy and a natural instinct for the visual close-ups which are so vital in film making. The vulnerability is there, but so is the sensuality and her obvious attraction for Nick despite her disarming come-backs. The scene was to acquire an off-camera significance never intended, for before the picture was released reports of a torrid affair between the two stars had found their way into the gossip columns, though according to many of those working on the set, little if anything untoward was evident during film making. None the less, it was well known that Barbra's marriage to Elliott Gould was not what it had once been, and she reportedly said that she found Sharif attractive. But again, what woman wouldn't?

If the press needed more they got it from an unexpected coincidence, for this so-called real romance between a highly charged actress from a traditional Jewish background and the latest dashing screen hero who happened to be a Lebanon-born Arab, occurred at the time of the Six-Day Arab-Israeli war. Barbra, never one to confide in the press or indeed to use the media excessively for her own ends, remained largely tight lipped, though one report had her admitting that she was in love with her handsome co-star.

Sharif was less restrained and spoke more openly about the affair which, he said, lasted during the making of the film. In that time, he said later in his own book, they had spent evenings and weekends together in her home '... we led the very simple life of people in love.' What is beyond dispute is that Streisand and Sharif went out openly together on dates, though that is by no means unusual for co-stars during the shooting of a film. But such rumours and reports tend to endure, to be passed down as gospel, and as recently as 1990 one UK national-circulation colour supplement talked about their 'sizzling love affair'.

In the picture that first kiss leads into the already-mentioned superb offering of 'People' with Streisand in excellent interpretative voice, her higher register phrasing swelling gloriously as she 'possesses' the song with an unmistakable attack and flair. Of the other musical offerings from *Funny Girl*, 'Don't Rain On My Parade', 'The Greatest Star' and of course the title song, there is the duet with Sharif 'You Are Woman, I Am Man', 'Second-hand Rose', an audition number for *Ziegfeld* with her appearance as gloriously smooth in a white close-fitting dress as her immaculate interpretation of the song, and her brilliantly extended and often underrated 'Sadie Sadie Married Lady' which she delivers with such verve, wit and style.

Of the musical numbers written specially for the film version, by far the more successful is the roller-skating sequence. It is also probably the most obviously funny scene in the picture. The definition of Streisand's humour is her natural instinct to laugh at herself. The comedy of the excellent bride scene is not only the visual impact of this very pregnant bride with the pillow stuffed up her front, but those glorious asides like her mock horror as she catches sight of herself in the mirror and, as she stands alongside those statuesque long-limbed *Ziegfeld* showgirls, the spontaneous grimace she produces to signify the contrast.

That these musical numbers gained much from the skills and experience of Herbert Ross, who had been brought in specially to direct them and with whom Barbra had worked when he had been choreographer on *I Can Get It For You Wholesale*, there is no doubt. And while Willie Wyler infuriated and frustrated both cast and crew with the constant changes he made, his perception in focusing on Streisand during the cutting and editing stages and strengthening the romance element between Fanny and Nick, was certainly vindicated at the box-office.

There is no doubt that Barbra's screen début and indeed the film itself, despite its critics, benefited from Streisand's interpretation of Fanny on stage. The change from the brash, youthful and at times unsure Brice in the earlier sequences, to the assurance and confidence of the more mature character later on as a *Ziegfeld* star, is handled with engaging finesse and subtle understanding by Streisand, the nuances apparent in delicately adapted body movements and the lack of the rasping Jewish–Brooklyn accent in the more sophisticated Brice.

The film set of *Funny Girl* seemed to yield a glut of rumour and innuendo, most of it perhaps a carry over from Barbra's reputation for being difficult to work with which she acquired during her stage work. The so-called scandalous affair between Streisand and Sharif had been preceded by reports of a bitter feud between the two. If the gossip writers couldn't get them one way, they'd have them another. There were plenty of reports that Barbra was uncooperative, meddled in production affairs which were none of her concern, was unfriendly, and isolated herself from other members of the cast. The Streisand–Wyler relationship was ripe for press speculation and exploitation. Certainly it all kept the picture in the public eye, however much or little of it was true.

Wyler dispelled many of the rumours and insinuations before giving a lecture at London's National Theatre shortly before his death at the age of seventy nine. He told Roald Rynning: 'I have worked with stars who tried to tell me how to direct, but I never had problems with Barbra as was rumoured at the time. We got on very well. She was interesting to work with. Not so easy. Not so difficult. She was completely absorbed in her work. And she had ideas.' The veteran director went on to explain that he and Streisand might agree on some of the ideas, or they might have discussions, differences. 'But our disagreements were also because we wanted the film to be marvellous.' He added: 'I remember her always being well prepared. I wouldn't be surprised if she stayed up all night reading the script because she always knew what to do. A total professional.'

Wyler explained that Barbra had specific ideas on how to play the part and fully accepted that, having been with the play so long, that she knew it better than anyone. 'It had been three

years of her life,' he said. 'Some of her ideas were good, some
not so good. I would rather direct someone who doesn't need to
be told what to do and where to move all the time, than an actor
not using his head.' And he told Rynning that the tale so often
repeated about him turning off his hearing aid every time she
came up with a suggestion, wasn't true. 'Barbra was interested
in every phase of the film, not just her own part,' he explained.
'She was always questioning everything, every detail about
making movies. But what's wrong with that? I welcome people
who take an interest in things. They are true professionals. We
watched the dailies [the previous day's filming] together, and
she knew every take, every scene, every line. It was a great help
to me. I had a marvellous time with Barbra, and that's the truth.'

Funny Girl broke new ground in being the first musical to
record a major production number live on film. Said Wyler:
'Usually the song is recorded first and then the artist mimes to a
play-back while being filmed. Upon viewing Barbra's performance of "My Man", which was the final song of the film, we
agreed that it needed to be more dramatic. It would be more
striking sung live. Then she could concentrate on the moment
instead of having to worry about lip synching.' He said that
Barbra always wanted to be convinced that what they were
doing was the best possible way. 'I could work her till she
dropped and she would never complain.'

Before leaving to deliver his lecture, Wyler told Rynning: 'I'm
terribly fond of her. She's a marvellous girl and a great
performer. *Funny Girl* was a very good experience for me.' And
Barbra it seems had fond memories of the experience, being
quoted later: 'It was wonderful having Wyler as my first
director. He wanted to show me off, that's why I came off so
well. To me he was like an audience. I got the feedback I
needed.' She was pictured much later giving him a fond hug at
the Hollywood opening of her tenth film, *A Star Is Born*.

Cynics might claim that time had made an old man
benevolent in his memories of a milestone in his career, but
whatever the absolute truth, there is no disputing the subtle
humour in their selection of gifts to each other at the time. At the
cast party at the end of the shooting Barbra gave Wyler an
antique eighteenth-century gold watch inscribed: 'To make up
for lost time'. Wyler's gift to his star was a director's megaphone
and a telescopic baton for conducting.

But not all members of the cast it seems shared Wyler's affection and admiration for the female star of the picture, certainly in her day-to-day attitude on the set and the power she reputedly exerted on the overall pitch and stance of the film. Anne Francis, who played Georgia, a *Ziegfeld* girl who befriends Fanny when she needs her most, apparently was not convinced that the hatcheting of many of her scenes was nothing to do with Streisand's influence. Her anger, frustration and disappointment was understandable, since some reports suggested that she would otherwise have been in the running for an Academy Award nomination for her supporting role. But in truth it is debatable if the undoubted influence of a Streisand would have been so all-powerful as to have been the reason for the cuts, – and, although Barbra's part in the end became much more dominant in the picture, she too suffered from the penal cutting of the film, her favourite *Swan Lake* ballet number being severely hacked.

Principal photography on *Funny Girl* was completed on 1 December 1967 and the première of the 147-minute movie was held at the Criterion Theater in New York on 18 September 1968. Barbra, in an eye-catching flowing gown and cape suited to such a glittering occasion, attended with Elliott to be greeted by thousands of enthusiastic fans who acclaimed their new star at the end.

The success of a lavish party afterwards was sealed by the early reviews, which were ecstatic for Streisand's performance. Her triumph and the huge box-office success of *Funny Girl* was all the more remarkable because it was being said in Hollywood that film musicals were beyond their peak as a genre. Barbra's sensational success was complete when later, at the Academy Awards ceremony, Ingrid Bergman stepped up to announce the winner in the Best Actress of 1968 category. There had been a good deal of competition and it was a tense moment as Bergman announced that there was a tie – and then, 'the winners are Katharine Hepburn and Barbra Streisand.' It was the only shared Best Actress award in Oscar history. Hepburn received the distinction for *The Lion In Winter*, although she wasn't present at the Oscar ceremony to receive her award.

Funny Girl was also to be significant in the parallels it was to hold within Streisand's own career. The similarities of Brice in terms of Streisand's characterization of her – the near obsession with perfection and the savage determination to make good in her career, were already evident in Barbra's own approach to her profession. Still to come was the painful break-up of her marriage (as Brice's had broken up) and the earlier compulsion in their love for Nick Arnstein, in Fanny's case, and Elliott Gould for Barbra. There were also to be true-life reflections in much of what Barbra was subsequently to do. The elements of passionate love and its disintegration, largely because of her husband's inability to live with a much more successful wife committed to an overtly devoted public and all the trappings of show-business success, the scenario of Barbra and Elliott in real life, was not only the basic formula of *Funny Girl*, but also of *A Star Is Born* eight years later. And who can deny that Barbra's obsession to see *Yentl* through whatever the cost in time, frustration, friendships and anxiety, as well as hard cash, did not result from her deep-rooted anguish and sense of personal emptiness she experienced through the loss of a father she never knew.

Funny Girl is probably unique for its staggering box-office success as a début picture. It grossed more than $26.5 million at a time when the influencial *Variety* was placing films with $4 million take into an 'all-time great' listing. Just consider what the picture might have made had it been released when film musicals were at their peak.

In taking the lead in the screen version of *Funny Girl* Barbra had run contrary to what was to become something of a Hollywood tradition, for movie history shows that stars of even massive stage successes seldom win the right to duplicate their triumph on film. But in Barbra's next film, *Hello Dolly!*, Hollywood worked the system in Streisand's favour, giving her the role in preference to Carol Channing, who had been an enormously successful Dolly Levi on Broadway. The story had lost some of its freshness by the time 20th Century Fox got around to committing it to film, for the stage musical, adapted from Thornton Wilder's *The Matchmaker*, had already featured such high-profile stars as Ginger Rogers, Betty Grable, Mary Martin and Ethel Merman. Even so, few could see producer and writer Ernest Lehman's logic in choosing the youthful Streisand for the role of the mature Dolly Levi more than twice her age.

News of the casting, released even before the start of filming on *Funny Girl*, had done little to win Barbra new friends. Critics

said she would be so miscast in the role, that she should have
turned it down and in accepting it was putting the chance to
earn big money before artistic principles. Certainly, when first
approached, Barbra could raise little enthusiasm for the part.
She thought Elizabeth Taylor would be a better choice and she
didn't much like the show anyway: 'When I first saw the show
on Broadway, I must say honestly I didn't like it and I never took
it seriously.' Nor did the moviemakers escape condemnation.
They were accused of wanting Streisand because it would make
a lot more money with her in it than anyone else, but Lehman
defended his choice, saying that he had considered Channing
before casting Streisand and had turned her down because he
felt that, after seeing her in *Thoroughly Modern Millie*, her
Broadway personality would not come over well on film. That
Barbra was miscast there can be little doubt, but financially the
picture wasn't the flop that many had anticipated. It grossed
more than $13 million which in many other circumstances
would have been considered extremely satisfactory. But against
the reckless and outrageously extravagant $20 million the film
cost to make, grossly excessive particularly for 1968, and
compared with the financial triumph of *Funny Girl*, it must rate
as a disappointment.

On the face of it, *Hello Dolly*! had everything going for it.
Against those critical of Streisand's casting, there were others
who, like Lehman, could well see Barbra in the role. Nor indeed
did Ernest Lehman's film pedigree at that stage justify too much
questioning, for he had written the screenplays for those two a
amazing blockbusters, *The Sound of Music* (where Julie Andrews
scored a huge success, taking over from Mary Martin who had
played Maria on stage) and *West Side Story*.

Roger Edens, a veteran and influential figure for some thirty
years for MGM during the period of those famous musicals, had
been brought in; Michael Kidd choreographed the picture; Jerry
Herman had produced what would arguably become his most
famous score and lyrics; and no less a figure than Richard
Zanuck, son of the legendary Darryl, who had taken over as
head of Fox, asked Gene Kelly to direct. Walter Matthau,
Michael Crawford and Marianne McAndrew were in the cast.
And just to make sure nothing could go wrong Louis
Armstrong, who had made *Hello Dolly*! a number-one hit in the
charts, was brought in to share the title song with Streisand.

Barbra at first didn't go along with this idea, maintaining that the scene should be strong enough to stand up on its own without resorting to a gimmick which, she believed, exploited Armstrong as well as cheapening the sequence and making it too obviously a commercial implant. But she changed her mind after the scene had been shot and saw how well it had all worked.

The film rights of *Hello Dolly!* were bought by 20th Century Fox in 1964, the year the show opened on Broadway, and their foresight and wisdom was more than justified when it went on to become the second biggest Broadway hit of all time, reaching 2,844 performances on Broadway and turning producer David Merrick into one of the most powerful men in show business.

In the filming of the famous tale, however, almost from the start things seemed to go wrong. The success of *The Sound of Music* was bringing a financial bonanza for Fox and, losing touch with reality on the strength of it, they failed to maintain sensible control of expenditure on *Dolly*. Securing the rights had cost them a basic $2 million but now their excesses became absurd. The sheer scale of their ambition was evident in the replica of New York's Fifth Avenue in the 1890s, which alone cost $3 million to construct, and reports have since put the number of extras engaged for Streisand's big number 'Before the Parade Passes By' at between 2,400 and 4,000. This scene, which included among other costly items like twenty-eight horse-drawn vehicles, a number of elaborate floats, and a reported eleven different marching bands, had to be shot again and again as technicians struggled with the nightmarish proportions of this critical sequence.

The on-set battles between Streisand and her co-star, Walter Matthau, began early in the shooting. Barbra's disposition to involve herself in aspects of the film which many felt to be of no concern to her, and her strongly held views which she expressed frankly and with vigour in pursuit of perfection, brought out the worst in the seasoned, irascible Matthau. After all, he was a veteran of a score of Hollywood movies and was twenty-two years Streisand's senior.

Something of the tension which had developed between them can be taken from Matthau's quote that he had no disagreements with Barbra Streisand: 'I was merely exasperated at her tendency to be a complete megalomaniac.' It all came to a head when Barbra was alleged to have made yet another of her

Going on seventeen. Barbara Joan Streisand on her graduation from
Erasmus Hall High School in 1959.

Having signed a 5-million dollar contract with CBS-TV to appear in a series of specials over the next decade, her debut in 1965 in 'My Name is Barbra' was a phenomenal popular success and gained five Emmy awards

Swinging with the greatest. A memorable guest spot on the Judy
Garland Show in 1963

'A Happening in Central Park'. Barbra's fear of live audiences had not yet fully developed. In these two photos she appears before an estimated 135,000 crowd in New York for a memorable televised public concert in 1967

Funny Girl grossed more than $26\frac{1}{2}$ million dollars and won Barbra an Oscar for Best Actress

Chorus line for *On a Clear Day* with Yves Montand, Sir Cecil Beaton, Alan Jay Lerner and Howard Koch

In 1968 *Funny Girl* made Barbra an overnight big-screen sensation and, in the words of the famous song from the movie, the greatest star

Ray Stark bought the film rights to a story by Arthur Laurents, intended as a vehicle for Streisand. The result brought golden star Robert Redford and Barbra together in the outstandingly successful *The Way We Were*

suggestions to director Gene Kelly, whose relative inexperience as a director and inherent good nature, made him too easy a target for the fiery Streisand, considered Matthau. He shouted: 'Why don't you let the director direct.' She retorted: 'Why don't you learn your lines,' striding off the set. Matthau insisted on having the last word – he shouted after her that everyone on the film hated her and that she ought to remember what happened to Betty Hutton, who once thought she was indispensable. This presumably was a reference to Hutton quitting Paramount at the height of her career when the studio refused to accept her new husband as the director of her next film, after which she made only one film, which was not successful.

The media rushed in to pick up the latest bit of studio gossip and *Life* magazine hinted that Barbra had a star complex as powerful as Joan Crawford's. To point up the analogy, Crawford had once been described by movie writer Ken Wlaschin as 'the screen's finest personificaion of no-holds-barred ambition ... who came to symbolize the bitch-goddess success, the dark side of the American dream.' It is doubtful if Matthau would have gone that far. Later, when Clive Hirschhorn was collecting material for a book on Gene Kelly, he interviewed Matthau, who added colour to the incident, admitting: 'I told her to stop directing the fucking picture, which she took exception to, and there was a blow-up in which I told her she was a pip-squeak who didn't have the talent of a butterfly's fart.' It is doubtful if Streisand, coming from Brooklyn, would be offended by Matthau's language; much more likely would she be upset by his public verdict on her ability as an actress.

Streisand took to staying in her trailer, spending much of her between-scenes time and off-duty moments with her baby son Jason, and in doing so gaining an unreserved and ill-deserved reputation perhaps for being aloof and unfriendly. There is no doubt that, although she had developed an enthusiasm for the picture, there must have been times during the bickering and in-fighting when she felt it couldn't end soon enough. And as time went on her original concerns about her being too young for the role must have returned. Personality clashes aside, it wasn't always easy in scenes with Matthau to see them as a natural pairing, Streisand's young, vibrant and sensual Dolly standing a little awkward against Matthau's more aged and subdued Horace Vandergelder. More than once she would telephone producer Ernest Lehman during the night to tell him she shouldn't really be in the picture.

Tensions rose as production costs soared. The film was never going to be successful through its story line alone, which was a rather meek tale of the middle-aged and meddling Dolly, widowed for ten years and spending her time and earning her living matchmaking, trying to ensnare Yonkers, New York merchant and 'well-known half-a-millionaire' Horace Vander-gelder (played by Walter Matthau) into becoming her second husband. Its visual impact, its scale on the big screen as a colourful extravaganza; Jerry Herman's memorable score including 'Put On Your Sunday Clothes', 'It Only Takes a Moment', 'Before the Parade Passes By' and the title song; and, above all, the characterization and sheer personality of Streisand as Dolly Levi, was what would count in the end: and to that extent Barbra was indispensable, as she had been in *Funny Girl*. Zanuck apparently told Matthau that whether or not Streisand thought herself indispensable, she was after a while, after the studio bosses had brought them to task and for the sake of the film, the pair co-existed in reasonable harmony, certainly so far as the outside world was concerned. Mellowed with the passing of time, years later a less cantankerous Matthau made amends for his acid comments: 'She was just too young for the part and she knew it. That's why she made it so difficult for everyone involved … I can see it now in perspective. She was a movie star, though none of her films had been released. She was insecure and she couldn't handle it.'

Almost for everyone involved, *Hello Dolly!* was not the happiest of films. Even when it was all over, the arguments and contradictions continued. Critical reaction was mixed and whether it was a success or failure depended very much on whom you spoke to. In *The Book of Musicals*, for instance, author Arthur Jackson said that the failure of *Hello Dolly!* was undeserved because in some ways he felt it was the best musical of the last decade. 'For one thing,' he wrote, 'it was based on a hit play [Thornton Wilder's *The Matchmaker*] and a worldwide hit on stage, earning the New York Drama Critics Award and no less than ten Tony Awards; while for another it was produced for the screen by Roger Edens, directed by Gene Kelly, choreographed by Michael Kidd, and scored by Lennie Hayton, each and every one a veteran of those same MGM musicals.'

And Jackson continued: 'And although she was miscast in the role of Dolly Levi, Barbra Streisand was still vibrant. *Hello Dolly!* demonstrated at least that star talent and behind-the-camera experience were still prerequisites for a classic Hollywood musical.'

To that extent, Ernest Lehman's opinion of Streisand which led to her being cast, or miscast, was apt, for he considered Barbra to be one of the most exciting talents to emerge in recent years. As for Barbra herself, she appears to have no definitive views about *Hello Dolly!* She largely kept her own counsel, not unusual for a Hollywood superstar who is also a very private person, laying the experience to rest once it was all over.

Perhaps the most unfortunate thing about the film, for its own reputation and for everyone concerned in its making, was the way David Merrick held back its release. Fox were compelled to keep the picture on ice until Merrick gave the go-ahead, a condition agreed by the film company at the outset, since Merrick was the producer of the successful Broadway presentation of *Dolly*. Who could blame him for withholding that permission, for the show was playing to packed houses. The Broadway show had been running for more than three years when Merrick gave the go-ahead for the picture to be released, but by then the audience for film musicals had gone.

The irony was that what David Merrick plainly gained on Broadway, he might well have lost out on Hollywood, for in addition to producing *Hello Dolly!* on stage, he was also a major stock holder in 20th Century Fox and thus missed out on the blockbuster the film might well have been had he given it the green flag earlier.

6 *Not Just the Singer*

Barbra Streisand has indicated more than once that the real joy in life for her is in reaching for an ambition. It far outstrips the satisfaction of achievement. As a gawky Brooklyn kid she wanted more than anything to become a star. And for her, that meant being up on the silver screen ... a movie star. After *Funny Girl* and *Hello Dolly*! she was certainly that, but having achieved what she had set out to do, how long would it be before her transitive nature would move her on to other challenges? After all, for someone who once said 'I can't go on singing "People" all my life,' the stimulus of doing something different meant more than sticking with a safe and winning formula. But, of course, she was already more than a movie star. She was a singing sensation and one of the highest-paid recording artists; a television personality; and when she could be persuaded to confront a live audience, she could name her own price for personal appearances.

In the end, the 1970s were to see her career moving ahead on all fronts, subtle changes extending her vision and satisfying that side of her Taurus temperament which made her recurrently capricious and mercurial. Musically she broadened her appeal by moving into the sphere of contemporary pop while in movies the 1970s would become her most prolific decade, with the release of no fewer than nine pictures. Here she measured herself against both light comedy and heavier drama, providing little opportunity for movie fans to enjoy her extraordinary musical talent until 1975, when she did *Funny Lady* for Columbia and, substantially more importantly despite its haranguing by the critics, *A Star Is Born*, a year later.

As the so-called 'Swinging Sixties' drew to an end there was no greater star than Barbra Streisand. She was picked out in one report as the 'new wonder of the age'. She had brought out an astounding seventeen LPs in a matter of months, made a devastating impact in two major movies, and while still only twenty seven, she became the only artist, male or female, to have won every major entertainment award. In a mere five years, she had done everything she had set out to do.

The Oscar which she won for her triumph in *Funny Girl* was reinforced by a Tony nomination for the same part. Her recording success and television specials brought her Grammy and Emmy awards, no other performer could match the multi-year, multi-million dollar contract she signed with Columbia, and she would herald a new decade by winning a Tony award in 1970 as 'the actress of the decade'. Before she was thirty, as James Spada was to point out, 'She had conquered Broadway, London, the recording industry, the concert circuit, television and finally and most triumphantly, Hollywood.' He declared that as a superstar in a generation otherwise without them, she was a star in the great tradition of stars, inspiring fierce loyalty and worship not seen since the days of Marilyn Monroe and Judy Garland.

Some idea of Streisand's enormous stature as an entertainer at this time and the particular magic she held for hundreds of thousands of fans, can be judged from the memorable public concert she gave in New York's Central Park in the summer of 1967. Only just twenty-five, she performed before an estimated audience of 135,000. For Streisand, superstar or not, this was a phenomenal achievement because never had she been thoroughly at ease before a live audience and a crowd of this size metaphorically turned her to stone. It was a prodigious undertaking and if it fell short of what many expected from this live 'happening', then perhaps it proved that the biggest star, superstar Streisand even, is human after all. The concert was in honour of New York itself, there was no charge for admission, and crowds began turning up at six in the morning for an estimated start time of 8 p.m.

Barbra was on her own, confronting a tension-packed situation highly charged with excitement and expectancy. With temperatures in the nineties, she paraded all the traditional favourites in a musical marathon which stretched to two-and-a-half hours. Edited down to an hour, it was well received when shown the following year on television, but live, on the night, it was a disappointment for many of her fans, some of whom walked away before the end.

Neither was she in top form when, after six years, she returned to Las Vegas, to the new International Hotel. Her $100,000 a week was reputed to be the biggest money ever paid to an entertainer in Las Vegas and in addition she would receive a significant shareholding in the new hotel. But, while Barbra felt this to be a time of transition in her professional career, with her moving on from the standard things which audiences expected of her, reaction was lukewarm to a performance which by even the most sympathetic assessment was uninspiring and too predictable.

Musical arrangements and her own interpretations of stock numbers which had not been updated, sounded too routine, and she failed to win over her audience. Her somewhat ordinary personal appearance on stage and her overall projection fell well short of the glitzy, colourful, even flamboyant performance expected by the Vegas audience from the world's top female entertainer. The critics came down heavily on her act, which upset her, and although later performances were to be much improved, this return to what many consider to be the premier entertainment centre of the world, was not the success everyone had hoped for and Barbra cannot have been too disappointed when her stint there ended.

She returned to Las Vegas late the following year, 1970, and made a further visit, to the International, now the Las Vegas Hilton, across the Christmas–New Year period, 1971-72. Both dates were highly successful and cancelled what lingering memories Barbra might have retained from the earlier visit. She appeared more relaxed and, having successfully travelled through a stage of transition to a more contemporary Streisand, gave performances which were appreciated even by the traditional Vegas audiences and generously received.

Life suddenly had become hectic for Streisand, whose string of titles and awards now included a second Golden Globe as 'World Film Favorite'. She had gone straight from the set of *Funny Girl* to her New York Central Park concert and, once back in Hollywood, was later to start work on her third film, *On a Clear Day You Can See Forever*. It had numerous pointers to success, even if the earlier Broadway show had been disappointing at the box-office. There was the creative score by the successful partnership of Alan Jay Lerner and Burton Lane, whose title song was to become a popular standard; production was in the capable hands of Howard W. Koch, production head at Paramount during 1965-66 and who was later to produce Neil Simon's classic comedy, *The Odd Couple*, starring Walter Matthau and Jack Lemmon; and Barbra asked for, and had succeeded in getting, the veteran Vincente Minnelli, one-time husband of Judy Garland, to direct.

Barbra played a dual role, as the confused American college student Daisy Gamble, and then as the elegant English eighteenth-century Lady Melinda Winifred Moorepark Tentrees, whose reincarnated identity Daisy reveals under hypnosis. The popular French singer and actor Yves Montand played Daisy's psychiatrist – a curious bit of casting perhaps since it was believed at the time that such luminaries as Frank Sinatra and Gregory Peck had been considered, while an emerging Jack Nicholson was down in the credits playing a small part as Daisy's half-brother. No less a personage than Sir Cecil Beaton, world famous for his royal and society photographic portraits since the 1920s, worked on the period costuming of the film. He had turned to costume design for ballet, theatre and films after the Second World War, and his outstanding work on *My Fair Lady* had brought him an Oscar.

The picture was enjoyable enough and if Streisand's performance seemed in some ways at odds, it was perhaps only in comparison with what had gone before – her portrayal of those larger-than-life characters Fanny Brice and Dolly Levi; while Montand, for all his Gallic charm and suitability for the part, didn't match the deeply smouldering persona of Omar Sharif, either on screen or off. Barbra didn't surprise anyone with her natural, easy characterization of Daisy, the sock-it-to-'em New Yorker, but her correct English accent in the Lady Tentrees sequences [she was coached by Deborah Kerr] was a delightful revelation. A disappointment for admirers of the Streisand singing voice was that some of the attractive songs by lyricist Alan Jay Lerner and composer Burton Lane went to Montand, though the title song was to become something of a Streisand special.

Unlike *Funny Girl* and *Dolly*, the picture was agreeable and companionable in the making with none of the high-tension dramas of Barbra's previous pictures. There were no fights with the director, no love affair with her co-star, and, so far as one can judge, no bitchiness among the cast. It appeared that Barbra, gaining from the experience of two major films, was more confident as well as relaxed, though she once again demonstrated her characteristic will for making every scene she was in as good as it possibly could be. She and Minnelli worked well together. She admired his directorial skills and had wanted him for her latest picture particularly because of his handling of the highly successful *Gigi*. He respected her ideas and views as a professional. He said later that he saw the relationship as more in the nature of a collaboration, rather than the director being the boss, though he added that he never agreed to anything which he didn't feel was good for the picture.

On a Clear Day is also well remembered for those delightful sequences when Barbra becomes reincarnated as Lady Tentrees, which were shot on location at Brighton, England, at the historic Royal Pavilion which George IV, when Prince Regent, had John Nash redesign in oriental style. These scenes, sumptuous through Beaton's costuming and set amid the pageantry and splendour of nineteenth-century English aristocracy, are among the most memorable in the picture. Even Beaton, not always easy to please, was impressed with what he and Barbra had accomplished. Interviewed shortly before his death in 1980, he recalled: 'There is perhaps no more overpowering visual and sensual scene (in the film) than the banquet. It was inspired – and both of our ideas really – to wrap the Streisand features in a glorious white turban, to further accentuate her strong features. At the same time she was totally feminine, beguiling, shamelessly sexual.'

The picture received good reviews and *Newsweek* was not alone in identifying Streisand in the dual role of Daisy Gamble and Melinda Tentrees as being an inspirational move. It was perhaps unjust that Montand received so much criticism, a good deal levelled at his somewhat heavy, and at times hard-to-understand, Gallic accent. Was it this reaction which goaded Barbra's co-star into accusing her of being responsible for reducing his role during the final cut?

This was one of only three blemishes on an otherwise happy and satisfactory production. Another was the character of Daisy who, some complained, was too well dressed and fashionable to be believable as a struggling college student. Her character, dressed in contemporary fashion by Arnold Scaasi, was filmed in Hollywood and New York. Finally was the somewhat disappointing public reaction to the film. The shooting ran over time a bit and in the end *On a Clear Day* cost some $10 million to make. This was a quite substantial sum for 1969 and it took some time, with the help of foreign rights and television sales, for it to get close to its original investment.

Whether this comparative indifference bothered Barbra is difficult to say, but in any event she had little time to ruminate. Before the end of 1969 she was back in a film studio, this time for her second picture for Columbia. Ray Stark had been casting around for a follow-up to *Funny Girl*, and eventually came up with a screenplay which couldn't have been more different. But *The Owl and the Pussycat* would provide Streisand with a new kind of challenge, testing her talent and extending her screen persona. The risk was evident. For one thing there would be no songs for Barbra to sing in this new picture. What would her fans say about that? And whether her public could ever reconcile her role as Doris, the hopeful model-cum-more-often-prostitute, with what had gone on before, only time would tell.

Barbra, however, shunned any such misgivings. She was eager, if quietly apprehensive. She needed to measure herself against this latest yardstick to her ability as an actress. Once again, it was the endeavour which counted most of all. But she did have some early misgivings about the sexual content of the movie and when she discovered that the role would require her to play her first nude scene, she was nervous and hesitant. 'I don't know what my mother will say,' she responded, taking the tension out of an unsure situation in a way which would have done credit to Fanny Brice in *Funny Girl*.

The story is of a book-shop assistant who has dreams of becoming a writer, an ingratiatingly diffident figure who is in the process of learning his limitations and enjoying life. The role was to provide a major break for the up-and-coming George Segal, whom Columbia had started to groom for stardom after he had shown certain promise as an engaging rogue in *King Rat* in 1965. Of the eleven films he had appeared in since then, *Who's Afraid of Virginia Woolf?*, *The St Valentine's Day Massacre* and *No Way to Treat a Lady*, in which he revealed an obvious talent for light comedy, were probably the best. *The Movie* assessed him as 'the master of matrimonial comedy, the keenest portrayer of romantic agony, domestic distress and confusion that the Seventies produced'. Herb Ross was brought in as director and Buck Henry produced the script with Segal and Streisand very much in mind.

Barbra didn't have to prove herself as an actress. She had done that convincingly enough in *Funny Girl* and indeed in *Hello Dolly!* Nor was she on trial as a light comedienne, because also she had proved her talent there. Her character in *The Owl and the Pussycat* meant she would have to work through a dialogue not short of an expletive or two, sexual innuendo, and whether she liked it or not, the script called for her to show more of her figure as the street-wise Doris Wilgus than in any of her previous films. Barbra liked the idea of not having to sing. It made the shooting less complicated and she could apply a single-mindedness to her scenes. It turned out to be a good film, funny and interesting from Barbra's point of view; and equally important, her fans accepted the new Streisand enthusiastically and the critics were impressed. The studio was delighted because it did very well at the box-office.

The co-stars got on well together and their relationship on-screen seemed to have that special something, an interaction which audiences can sense if unable to define. Segal praised her without qualification – easy to work with, warm, a real professional. He also said she had an unerring instinct, a comment especially interesting in view of Robert Redford's view, after working with her in *The Way We Were*, released in 1973, that she didn't see the business of acting in such an intuitive way as he did. The picture was certainly important to Barbra's career because it established her convincingly as a non-musical actress and, although the first, was to be decidedly the best of four light-comedy movies she would do in the 1970s. She was sensitive, showed skill in handling comedy and didn't dominate the picture as she had done in her previous movies. That could be a disappointment, depending on your point of view and how deeply you are under the Streisand spell, but the critics thought it a move in the right direction, taking it as a sign of growing experience and maturity in front of the camera. Some still consider it among the best films she has done.

She now saw herself ready to extend further into drama, but a number of circumstances worked against it. By 1972 Peter

Bogdanovich had built up a sound reputation as a film maker who used nostalgia as a key element in his success, linking pertinent themes with earlier films. The year before he had scored a major triumph with *The Last Picture Show*, about a number of young people trapped in their home town and saddened by the closure of their local cinema.

Barbra was keen to do a film with him, but having just done *Picture Show*, Peter was intent on doing a comedy. Barbra was also keen to set up a picture with Ryan O'Neal, still basking in the glory of the multi-million dollar box-office success, *Love Story*, in which he co-starred with Ali MacGraw.

To bring all the essential threads together takes us back to the end of the 1960s. After the success of *The Owl and the Pussycat*, Streisand had insisted on taking some time off and for more than a year she stayed away from movies, concentrating on being a mother and enjoying being close to Jason. At the same time husband Elliott Gould's acting career was taking off. He was featured in a clutch of good films and two of them, *Bob & Carol & Ted & Alice* in 1969 and *M*A*S*H* a year later, were to become huge hits. But by now he and Barbra had long since given up all hope of a reconciliation and before Streisand was ready for her next picture she was already going out with O'Neal. Hence her desire to do a movie with him.

The only problem, it seemed, was that Bogdanovich insisted on doing a comedy and, being Bogdanovich, looked to the past for inspiration. In Streisand he detected a modern-day Jean Arthur or Carole Lombard and putting everything together came up with the idea of doing an old-fashioned, screwball comedy based on the type of movie popular with Hollywood in the 1930s. Bogdanovich was happy with that, Ryan O'Neal was happy with it, so two out of three wasn't a bad proportion and Barbra gave up her idea of doing a drama and settled for *What's Up Doc?*

Some commentators still consider it to be not only the best comedy Streisand has made, but also one of her very best films. For many others, however, its most redeeming feature was Barbra's singing of 'You're the Top' behind the opening and closing titles, and the merest snatch of 'As Time Goes By' half-way through. Released in 1972, this Warner Brothers picture was described by *The Movie* as a 'high-style screwball with a big star and an intricate plot which involves a madcap girl running around San Francisco trying to seduce a young musicologist, but in doing so she unavoidably gets them both caught up in a series of slapstick adventures.' The assessment went on: 'The film never faltered with its set-pieces and Barbra Streisand was as warm and unmannered as she has ever been.'

After working with Barbra on her first four films, her favourite cameraman had died and she now turned to Laszlo Kovacs, one of Hollywood's most versatile and gifted cinematographers, specially skilled in creating a mood and an atmosphere. Buck Henry was called in to work on the script and shooting began in the summer of 1971. There were no tantrums on the set, though as usual Barbra insisted on knowing how Bogdanovich planned to work every scene she was in and often contributed her own ideas. Barbra, however, was said to be aloof and her unpunctuality on the set was vexing. She and O'Neal worked well together, but although the picture was to win immediate success after its release at Easter 1972, bringing Barbra the title of 'Box-office Champ of the Year' and the claim by one critic that it was even better than *Funny Girl*, Barbra wasn't happy with the result.

She said later that she didn't believe the basic material was substantial enough for her, a view with which viewers of recent television repeats of the picture are likely to agree, and that she didn't enjoy making the movie. Her romance with Ryan O'Neal didn't last the picture out, though making it together didn't account for their parting. A liaison with Peter Bogdanovich had taken over, but this apparently didn't alter the strong control he kept on production. According to Austin Pendleton, who took the part of Frederick Larrabee in the picture, Bogdanovich was a very strong director. He said in an interview with Peter Cosenza for *All About Barbra*: 'He didn't allow any interference from his actors, so any rumours about Barbra running the show are unfounded. He called the shots.' Pendleton said he never felt awestruck around Barbra '… simply because she's so natural, so real, so down-to-earth. Off-camera though she can be a lot like she is on the screen. For instance she talks very fast in person just like in her movies. She uses a lot of herself in her performances.'

On the strength of her performances in *The Owl and the Pussycat* and *What's Up Doc?* there were reports of all kinds of major projects being lined up for Streisand. In the United States she had been the tenth biggest box-office draw in 1969 and ninth in 1970; strongly rumoured now was what would have become her greatest challenge yet, the life of Sarah Bernhardt, to be directed by the controversial, flamboyant, British-born Ken Russell. It would not be the last time such reports circulated, but the hotly anticipated project didn't happen, not even into the 1990s.

No satisfactory explanation was announced. Perhaps Russell's own developing eccentricities – in 1971 in *The Music Lovers* he had the traditional image of Tchaikovsky as a romantic composer shockingly contrasting with Russell's own projection of him as a homosexual seized by emotional conflict – perhaps was something of a put-off, even for Streisand. But this was still no time for fans desperate for Barbra to do another musical to celebrate. Her career was still in a period of self-induced transition and by now she had more control over the films she did. Big names on screen were getting more involved with the whole process of film selection and film making, not just acting, and two years before Barbra had formed First Artists, a film partnership with Paul Newman and Sidney Poitier (later to be joined by Steve McQueen and Dustin Hoffman), as an extension of her production company Barwood, which she had earlier established with Elliott Gould.

Barbra saw her next role as an ordinary, everyday woman devoid of eccentricities, and was intrigued by the possibilities of a novel which a friend had first sent to her. She bought the screen rights and set up plans to make her sixth film in five years. *Up the Sandbox* might well have seemed trivial after the rumours about Sarah Bernhardt and Ken Russell, and would once more disappoint her musical-starved fans, but Barbra was herself enthusiastic about the project. Her character, Margaret Reynolds, is a Manhattan housewife looking after her husband and two children, who finds that this is no longer enough to satisfy her life. Rather than do something positive about it and leave the family she loves, she indulges in a series of harmless exotic fantasies which range from pushing her mother's face into an anniversary cake after telling her frankly what she thinks about her, to travelling to Africa to learn about painless child birth and confronting the Cuban dictator Fidel Castro at a press conference. In contrast, Margaret's real life becomes even more humdrum and when she becomes pregnant she is tempted to have an abortion, but decides against it.

A successful picture would benefit Barbra financially, since she was reportedly set to make ten per cent of the gross profit and one third of the net profit. She was enthusiastic and optimistic, at first marginally torn between producing the picture and acting in it, but with a shooting start date in March 1972 and sound stages booked at 20th Century Fox studios, she settled into the part of Margaret Reynolds, being content to keep an eye on production after persuading Irwin Kershner to direct. David Selby was cast as Margaret's husband.

Barbra had known Kershner since shortly after making *Funny Girl* when, after receiving a note congratulating her on her performance, she had invited him over to her home for tea. Later he would become best known for directing *The Empire Strikes Back*, with Harrison Ford, Mark Hamill and Carrie Fisher, in 1980.

David Selby was new to movies and had never met Streisand before the start of the picture, but would make a solid reputation for himself later through television soaps *Flamingo Road* and, in particular, *Falcon Crest*. It would be a distinction and a unnerving responsibility perhaps for the unknown to be working with such a superstar and you can take your pick from numerous reports which suggest he was overawed by it and his own assessment that he wasn't. He said he did not feel intimidated opposite Streisand; he was just being quiet and observing a lot.

Certain scenes were shot in New York, where Barbra celebrated her thirtieth birthday and went sight-seeing around some of the old haunts. The picture also gave her the opportunity to visit East Africa, where one of Margaret's wilder dreams was shot. Some critics would wonder if it had been absolutely essential to picture primitive, tribal women bare-breasted, and it was breasts again which provided the picture with perhaps its most bizarre fantasy.

In order to divert her husband's wandering eye, Margaret grew enormous breasts. Talking about the sequence afterwards Barbra said it was very technical and felt grotesque. 'I was rigged up with balloons and pipes, two men for each boob and one for the stomach. It took forever,' she said. Kershner found Barbra pleasant and co-operative to work with, remembering only one occasion when she threatened not to do the film and went home, but she was back next morning. Even then

Kershner reckons he was to blame for pushing too hard. He admires Streisand immensely, considers her to be grossly maligned in his experience, and said she was wonderful to work with. It was he, for instance, and not Streisand as some of her critics have suggested, who insisted on Barbra being the only major star among a cast of unknowns. He wanted to tone down Barbra's superstar quality and it would have been foolish to replace one superstar, as it were, with another.

The picture is also notable for the fleeting movie début of Jason Gould, playing on a carousel, and Barbra was overjoyed that she was able to take him with her on safari to Kenya for the sequences already mentioned ... along with, according to reports, a secretary, two friends and eighteen suitcases.

If Kershner was surprised not to encounter problems with Barbra in the making of *Up the Sandbox* – he had anticipated them from what he had read and been told about her, he certainly wasn't happy with the script and story line. A Pulitzer Prize winner, Paul Zindel, had been hired to turn the book into a film, but Kershner was doubtful if the book would lend itself convincingly to the drama treatment required for a movie. He almost didn't take on the project for that very reason, only the opportunity of working with Barbra made him decide to go ahead. Though this difficulty presented problems during the shooting, he reckoned Barbra's presence in the picture and the stronger dimension her performance gave to it, would outweigh the problems and he fully expected the picture to be a hit.

But unfairly, as some would say, it wasn't by any means a commercial success. Despite Barbra's unusual decision to promote the picture in late December, 1972, further press conferences and her presence at a charity première in New York just before Christmas, the hopes that attended its release over the Christmans season were never fulfilled. Box-office receipts ran fractionally over $4 million, well below what was required, with subsidiary rights and sales including video, to bring Barbra any kind of profit.

Reasons advanced for the failure ranged from the picture's shortcoming in not pitching for a clear-cut market segment – too old-fashioned for hardcore feminists and too revolutionary for ordinary housewives ran one assessment – to the restricting censorship category it picked up, unfairly asserted Streisand later, because of the bare-breasted sequences. 'What kind of

morality do you have when people would rather have children
see blood and gore than a woman's breast,' she stormed.

It has to be said, and has been freely admitted by Streisand and
Kershner, that as the picture developed it was not always clear
when Margaret was herself and when she was fantasizing; nor
were its chances enhanced because of the public's basic misconception. They had expected it to be another slapstick comedy in
the style of her last picture, *What's Up Doc?*, and here surely the
advertising and promotional approach for the picture was tacti-
cally at fault, graphics and illustrations trying to tease the punters
into another fun picture.

Its failure aside, Barbra didn't regret doing the film. It gave her
for the first time the hands-on experience of being involved in
pictures in ways other than in front of the camera, and in a
professional sense she found it satisfying and fulfilling. She
learned lessons too, appreciating as never before the production
difficulties in film making, but she also enjoyed the considerable
satisfaction of being perceived for the first time by many
reviewers and critics as a serious actress of some significance.

But surely the final irony was this: Alan and Marilyn Bergman
had collaborated with Billy Goldenberg on a theme song for the
picture called 'If I Close My Eyes', which was intended to be run
under the final credits. In an effort to staunch a flagging box-
office this fully orchestrated vocal was sacrificed in favour of the
basic simplicity of the tune, played on a toy piano with vocals.

One abiding happy memory of the picture for Barbra, however,
was of her visit to East Africa, in which she delighted. As reported
by Donald Zec and Anthony Fowles in *Barbra – A Biography of
Barbra Streisand*, 'Barbra was fascinated by the costumes and
exotic make-up of the ultra-beautiful Senegalese women. At one
point she asked one of them to put some of the dancer's blue eye
make-up on her own eyelids.' Later Zec and Fowles explain:
'Streisand and the dancers ... gave each other the freedom of the
wardrobe. Streisand, as excited as a child, allowed herself to be
costumed, necklaced and turbaned in the style of an African
princess.'

Sandbox brought Streisand an unexpected financial failure, the
first to that extent in a six-picture, five-year period, but if the
experience was demoralizing – though that is hardly likely, then
within a little more than a year she would be enjoying her greatest
success to that time – a complete turnabout.

Robert Redford, five years Streisand's senior and a fast-emerging Hollywood star with golden-boy looks and a sardonic, clean-cut image, was to be her co-star in her latest film, titled *The Way We Were*. Credit for starting the whole thing off once again must go to Ray Stark, along with Arthur Laurents. The latter had written the story as a vehicle for Streisand and the book was still unpublished when Stark bought the film rights, before Barbra had begun filming *What's Up Doc*? This latest picture, to be directed by Sydney Pollack, didn't much interest Redford to start with, but once Pollack had worked with writers David Rayfield and Alvin Sargent to give additional depth to the male lead, it was more the kind of part to attract Redford.

The story set out as an old-style romantic melodrama, described by David Downing in his book on Robert Redford, as 'man and woman joining together and falling apart to the accompaniment of the string section and much muffled sobbing in the back stalls'. More helpful perhaps was this outline from Clive Hirschhorn in *The Hollywood Musical*, where Barbra is seen 'in what was surely her best dramatic role ever ... as a radical girl in love with the very square Robert Redford...'.

The added dimension to the new film would be the mixing of the traditional story into a background of American politics in the years following the end of the Second World War, with developing backdrops from the innocence of the pre-war college campus to the pernicious anti-Communist witch-hunts in a disturbed Hollywood during the days of the Cold War. Streisand plays Jewish girl Katie Morosky, Redford is Hubbell Gardiner and after being at college together they meet again some time later during the war in a New York bar where Hubbell shows signs of having had more than just a couple of drinks.

The picture then moves into an extended flash-back with the two contemporaries at college, Katie as a militant left-wing agitator and Hubbell filling the role of the all-American boy who puts politics well down the list of priorities. But they each find the other irresistibly attractive, despite their opposing views, and Katie is impressed when she finds out that he is considered to have a bright future as a talented writer. Once back in the present that mutual attraction is consummated. The relationship develops and in the fulness of time, and with the war over, we find them married and living in Hollywood, where Hubbell is busy adapting a successful novel he has written into a movie story.

The Way We Were has its tenser moments as the power that draws the two opposites together also pushes them painfully apart. Their love for one another endures to the end, but fate and circumstances divide them as Katie becomes involved in the campaign against the McCarthy blacklist. With the breakdown of their marriage comes the eventual realization that they can never survive emotionally and psychologically – or in reality – as a couple.

The perverse nature of film-making was never better demonstrated than in Barbra's two movies, *Up the Sandbox* and *The Way We Were*. The former had been expected to do well at the box-office and had been planned and created within an atmosphere of confidence. In the end the public were not impressed and the film has gained nothing with the passing of time. *The Way We Were*, on the other hand, was never really considered as an exciting prospect. Columbia Pictures bosses had considerable misgivings – and their nervousness was understandable since they agreed to do the picture at a time when their balance sheet showed the company some $200 million in the red – and even after shooting had started they would probably have aborted the project given the chance. For six months Robert Redford fought against doing the picture. The story line, with its backdrop of Communism and political witch-hunt, wasn't a natural subject to appeal to a mass audience. Yet the picture was an outstanding hit, saved Columbia Pictures from financial catastrophy, and over the years has emerged as a genuine classic of its kind.

Few would deny that in *The Way We Were* Streisand gives a compelling performance. Those previously critical of her for what they claim to be her theatrical and musical comedy mannerisms and overplay were happy and impressed to see her back to what director Sydney Pollack described as the 'simple truth' performance he knew her to be capable of. It was considered in many quarters to be one of the best romantic films of those years.

There were a number of memorable scenes and Barbra's passionate performance brings Katie uncannily close to home. One of the finest, in Streisand chronicler Allison J. Waldman's opinion, is the picture's first love scene. 'When Katie climbs into bed with the drunken Hubbell and he makes love to her in a daze, it's just incredible,' assesses Waldman. 'Pollack's camera stays tight on Barbra's face through most of the scene as she runs a gamut of emotions – from the initial daring of wanting him to reach for her, to the unfulfilled desire when he goes through the motions automatically, to the final despair and sadness when she says softly: "Hubbell, it's Katie. You did know it was Katie".'

The same writer also favours the scene of confrontation between Katie and Hubbell in the train station when she comes back from Washington, reportedly written by David Rayfield to delineate the polarization of Hubbell and Katie on the subject of politics. 'The power of the Streisand and Redford combination in this fight scene is electric, as they both hold their ground, each arguing a valid, opposing point with all their emotions and convictions on the line,' says Waldman, who considers that the only scene to top it is the finale which, in her view, is 'simply a classic'.

The Way We Were was not alone in having its finale rewritten. The debate centred around the resolution of their diametrically opposite views after Hubbell's job at the film studio is threatened because of Katie's subversive activities. The choice then is whether this is ultimately a love story or whether the powerful strand of political conscience will win through. There were no shortage of views expressed and several endings were shot, the idea that the political viewpoint should triumph by no means being ignored.

In these versions, including one where Katie faces the problem and voices the solution with the dispassionate comment 'There's a very easy answer ... we'll get a divorce,' Barbra's performances, according to director Sydney Pollack, are outstanding. Creating the right balance between the political strands of the film and the love story element was a headache for Pollack who freely admits the picture's lack of complete success in this respect, especially in the middle and later stages.

While reducing the film's value in purist terms, the powerful yet sensitive portrayals from both Redford and Streisand more than made up for any possible script deficiencies at a more popular level. Whether the solution to the ending problem is fundamentally convincing or is satisfactory to those involved in making the picture, is immaterial in a sense as audiences are left to make up their own minds as Hubbell, facing the dilemma, drifts back to a former love, Carol Ann (played by Lois Chiles). When Katie sees this happen she realizes that the marriage is ended and agrees to a divorce after their child is born. After that, what is perhaps the inevitable ending, is enacted when Hubbell and Katie meet unexpectedly in New York years later. Their embrace is loving and tender and they both realize that their feelings for one another have not diminished over the years. At the same time they recognize the impossibility of a life together.

Some twenty minutes or so of the film was eventually to be cut, but the ending to be finally chosen by Pollack, while displeasing the original author Arthur Laurents, who favoured a stronger political slant, was surely vindicated on the basis that *The Way We Were* was above all else an absorbing and heart-rending love story and not a political drama *per se*. This was surely to be confirmed when the picture outshone all others to become without any doubt, the love picture of the year. *The Way We Were* was to become one of the most famous and best loved of all Streisand films. The pairing of Streisand and Redford was an inspiration. They were perfectly matched and their performances were breathtaking. The censor was snap-happy in cutting the film excessively, but the video version put out subsequently by RCA/Columbia had the additional feature of being uncut and, in many a critic's view, is all the better for it.

The making of the picture didn't suffer the high-tension dramas and emotional 'stand-offs' of some of Streisand's earlier offerings. Barbra continued her late-night calls to director Sydney Pollack, her mind full of possibilities and doubts about her portrayal and how things would work out on the following day's shooting, and she was concerned that wherever possible she should be photographed from her best side. Curiously, this coincided with Redford's worst side and how that particular situation was overcome is anyone's guess, though doubtless it would call for a high degree of diplomacy from Pollack and a measure of good will on the part of the co-stars.

It was a happy development for Barbra that the son of Harry Stradling, who had photographed her first four films and whose work she had admired so much, was at work on her latest picture, and she praised Redford's performance, being impressed by his outstanding ability to underact the part with gestures which were more powerful than words. Her determination to stick to principles she felt important was still strongly evident. She didn't hesitate to complain that Pollack had Katie crying too much and never did get over her favourite scene being cut out of the picture altogether. She maybe felt she ought to have been more assertive and certainly it was incidents of this kind which made her determined to have more overall control when she got the opportunity in 1976 with First Artists' decision to go ahead with a remake of *A Star Is Born*. In less important areas she got her own way. She insisted for instance in retaining her long finger nails and she wore her own hair whereas in most of her other films she used a wig.

The picture had its flaws. At times it appeared disjointed and was not all that easy to follow, with the plot seeming to become somewhat confused in terms of time scales. Some critics were disturbed because they considered the story had been given a pro-Communist slant, though a close analysis hardly bears out the criticism. There was general feeling, however, that the picture had given Streisand her best dramatic role ever.

Despite the parlous state of Columbia at the time, confirmation for the film to go ahead had been given in April 1972 and shooting started in August that year. An early preview took place in late October the following year to an enthusiastic reception and the film went out on general release on 23 October 1973. Columbia had nervously set a $5 million budget for the picture and became extremely worried as they saw the bill rising menacingly above that figure. But heavy frowns turned to broad smiles because within three months of its release the picture had grossed over $30 million and was to go on to become one of the most popular successes ever recorded by Columbia. It reached the number-one spot in the United States and received Oscar nominations for best actress, best cinematography, best art direction, best costume design, best song and best original dramatic score.

The haunting title melody, composed by Marvin Hamlisch with lyrics by Marilyn and Alan Bergman, won an Oscar, a second Oscar being awarded for the best score. Barbra missed out as the best performing actress that year, by what must have been the narrowest of margins, the Oscar going surprisingly to Glenda Jackson for *A Touch of Class*. But she enjoyed some consolation later when her recording of the evocative and beautifully lyrical title song became her first number-one single, bringing her also a Grammy and a Golden Globe. Some idea of the disappointment Barbra must have felt at missing out on the Oscar could be judged some years later when, though rarely responding to enquiries about her personal feelings, she admitted: 'I felt I deserved that award. I felt my performance was the best of the five nominated that year.'

The picture's outstanding success none the less must have begged the inevitable question about a follow up. And why not? For, as some members of the original crew facetiously commented, there must have been enough of the original left on the cutting room floor to get a sequel off to a flying start. Streisand might have been persuaded, but Redford was never keen on the idea. However, even as late as 1985 the idea didn't seem completely lost for, when talking to the *Salt Lake City Desert News*, Robert Redford revealed: 'I guess it's a possibility. I'm the least enthusiastic about it. You could do something in this you couldn't do in other films. You could have Barbra and me at our own ages, twelve years later. And you could use the original movie for flash-backs.'

Even more recently came reports that Ray Stark was trying to put together an $18 million project for a sequel to *The Way We Were*. But Redford told *Premiere Magazine*: 'There are too many things to do to go back and do a sequel and repeat. I think *The Way We Were* would make a very good sequel, but I don't want to do it.' But he added that he had also refused to do the original when it was first put to him.

At the same time, for fans desperate to see Streisand and Redford together again, there was more hopeful news as the two were linked in a possible venture by United Artists who were looking to bring author Pat Conroy's *The Prince of Tides* to the screen. But, as is now known, when the project eventually became reality and shooting began in 1990 with Barbra as both director and producer, and co-starring with Nick Nolte, there was no Robert Redford in the cast list. It appears that the possibility of a re-match is increasingly remote.

Returning to their original success, Streisand got on extremely well with Redford and there was none of the verbal mud-slinging which Barbra had experienced from Walter Matthau. Both Barbra and Redford have strong personalities and definite views when making a film, but while these did not always coincide, Redford found no difficulty in working with Barbra and discovered her somewhat fearsome reputation unfounded. 'Barbra was not the fighter I'd heard – not any kind of bitch.' He said he found working with her stimulating and while she wasn't easy going ... we got along fine.' Redford was probably Barbra's most enjoyable co-star. They were friendly, played a bit of tennis together, and were companionable. Barbra thought he was not only a mature and thinking actor, but outstandingly good looking and exciting as a person. Writer Arthur Laurents, as reported by James Spada, said that a great deal of the sexual chemistry of those early scenes was quite real. The gossip writers tried to develop stories of a romance between the two, but, although their friendship was in many ways close during the filming, their relationship was nothing more than that.

In any event, towards the end of shooting Barbra would soon meet Jon Peters, with whom she would develop a steady relationship, but the fact that she had been seen in public with a number of dates in recent years made her an easy and persistent target for sections of the press interested in reporting and speculating on such detail. Her marriage to Elliott Gould had finally ended on 9 July 1971 when they were given a divorce in the Dominican Republic. It was the official sanction to end a marriage which had existed in name only for some time and although in many respects she and Elliott were to remain quite friendly, there was never to be any suggestion of a reconciliation.

Barbra, never denying that she enjoyed the company of her choice of eligible men, had formed attachments, as indeed had Elliott, before their marriage ended. She and Ryan O'Neal had dated discreetly before the news got to the press and after that she became friendly with Peter Bogdanovich. Her official release from Elliott put the press on red alert and they rumoured her, as a newly available 'single', as having a variety of romances. Their obsession with Barbra's private life, not unnaturally perhaps, had begun earlier and from about 1969 onwards she would be successively reported to be going out with men as different in outlook, character and stature as Anthony Newley, Warren Beatty and George Lazenby, not to mention sundry others not connected with the film business and therefore unknown to the general public.

Doubtless the most public of her liaisons happened in early 1970 when the then Prime Minister of Canada, Pierre Trudeau – himself highly eligible and extremely handsome, became captivated by her. Like it or not, politics became involved with show business at the highest level during a now well-documented incident in the Canadian Parliament. With Streisand present in the public gallery, Trudeau's attention was not apparently fully on the proceedings, a situation which drove Mr George Hees, a member of the opposition, to address the Prime Minister thus: '... if the Prime Minister can take his eyes and mind off the visitors' gallery long enough to answer.' It was an embarrassing and humiliating incident for everyone concerned and is likely to have contributed to the ending of the romance between these two highly motivated, high-profile personalities.

They had first met in London at the film première of *Funny Girl* and were together again during a Commonwealth Prime Ministers' Conference there. Trudeau, a French Canadian, was the most dashing of the international politicians, with a trendy profile highlighted by his young wife, Margaret. But after a number of highly publicized estrangements, the couple were finally to separate in 1977. His friendship with Barbra, consolidated with public dates in New York, was further 'scandalized' by their difference in age – he was fifty one in 1970, she twenty eight, and the Canadian public showed growing concern as the relationship showed every indication of becoming serious. Trudeau didn't help matters when, confronted with pertinent questions on nationwide television, his hostile and disdainful reply left the interviewer in no doubt that he, Trudeau, believed that his relationship with Streisand was none of his, the interviewer's, or the public's business.

In a later *Playboy* interview, Barbra, while dodging the central question 'Did he ask you to marry him?', did admit to speculating on what it might have been like had their relationship further developed and she had become the first lady of Canada: 'I thought it would be fantastic. I'd have to learn how to speak French. I would do only movies made in Canada. I had it all figured out. I would campaign for him and become totally politically involved in all the causes, abortion and whatever.'

That scenario wasn't to be, but as her career advanced Barbra

Streisand was to become politically involved in other ways as her concerns for the way of life, the environment and the protection of the earth's natural resources made an increasing impression on her consciousness.

7   A Very Singular Lady

By the mid-1970s Barbra Streisand's public persona was clearly defined. She had established herself as one of the most electrifying performers on the big screen and was hugely successful as a live entertainer and recording artist. She was in a class of her own at her own special brand of comedy and had proved herself, to the surprise of many of her critics, as an impressive serious actress. Her phenomenal singing voice, with its over two-octave range, was combined with a singularly consummate style to make her genuinely unique and for many the most exciting popular singer of the day.

For all that, however, she was largely misunderstood as a person. She had acquired a fearsome reputation as a man-eater, noted for her particular style of feminism. Some claimed her impossible to work with, self-centred to the point of megalomania. Yet adding to the dilemma and complexity of the real Streisand were those who would equally refute the allegations, some from working closely with her on a picture. What is certain is that Barbra Streisand is an exceedingly complex being with a duality of personality which defies simple analysis. That she has often been at odds with the media hasn't helped the public to get to know the real Streisand. She is fiercely dedicated to her own ambitions and ideas, yet at times surprisingly vulnerable to persuasion and manipulation. She can be forceful and incredibly sensitive; bold yet insecure; supremely confident in one situation, nervously infantile in another. Her purity of voice and matchless technique will send rivers of tingling emotion rushing up and down the spine in one song; in the next she can be strident, vocally inept and tasteless.

She is the kind of performer who sends moderate views scampering to extremes. There is seldom any middle ground. You either love her singing or hate it. Her fans will travel miles to see her latest picture; others couldn't be prised out of the house to see her. She has been labelled plain and even ugly, yet for many she has an attraction and sensuality which lavishly transcends the mere acceptable concepts of beauty.

Surprisingly little is known about the real Barbra Streisand. Despite all the interviews, studio gossip, press handouts and comments from associates claiming to have rumbled her complex character and personality, Barbra over the years would become irritated and incensed as she felt herself to be increasingly maligned and misunderstood, while the public was left to pick its own way through a minefield of often conflicting views and information.

Certainly, it isn't easy to sort out the real Streisand. For a start she is so changeable that the impression she can create one moment isn't necessarily reliable for another time. But to begin to get at what one publication labelled the 'stunning super-truth' of Barbra, it doesn't do any harm to go back to her birth.

Born on 24 April makes her a Taurean – said to be thrifty with a methodical streak and with a love of beauty, food and luxury. Not too unlike Streisand perhaps, but Taureans are also prone to hold on to what they have and are seldom extravagant. According to the astrological charts, they are affectionate and sensual, but may get stuck in a rut and become possessive, boring and self-centred.

There is nothing too much to quarrel with in that broad assessment of Barbra's Taurean character. She is also a Friday's child which, according to legend, makes her 'loving and giving' – an assessment with which even now her erstwhile husband Elliott Gould would be disinclined to argue. At a factual level, Barbra Streisand is smaller than is often realized, about 5ft 4in is one given estimate, and has maintained a bodily beauty which she herself scorns when faced with such a feminist viewpoint, and which the media has generally not noticed or has elected to ignore in favour of her more controversial features. Her hands are expressive and exceptionally elegant, her neck exquisite. Her movies have provided ample evidence of her stylish walk and physical presence. Never a body-cult personality, Streisand none the less has been shown to have a good figure, with long, slim legs, full breasts and, as lover Jon Peters observed at the beginning of their relationship, 'a cute ass'. He also remarked on how surprised he was that she was little and petite and had a pretty body.

She is not a classical beauty, but the sum of the imperfections somehow produces an outstandingly attractive face, particularly when framed with a becoming hairstyle. She has a beautiful skin, her eyes are large and expressive, her lips fetchingly generous, and the shape of her face is congenial and harmonious. Her gaze, on the evidence of her numerous films, can be searching and devastating. The personality which lights up her being with an abundance of emotions made her one of the most striking and exciting of people, both on and off the screen.

Coffee ice-cream was an obsession during her early, struggling days in New York and her increased sophistication and enormous prosperity has by no means transformed her into a natural gourmet. Her taste in food and drink has reportedly broadened over the years, though it is said that she still enjoys ice-cream and is tempted by her life-long passion for rice pudding, pop-corn and Cola. She has a naturally good appetite and is inclined to put on a few ounces, but according to those close to her who should know, she looks her best when she is slimmer. Twice when she has been in Britain she has visited the exlusive Champneys Health Resort, situated in beautiful grounds in Hertfordshire. On one occasion she had to leave prematurely because word got around that she was there and the media besieged the place, but reports from some of those who looked after her there indicated that she was a model guest.

Barbra would be the first to admit that she is not a natural-born intellectual, yet the brash Brooklyn background which has tended to persist in a widespread view of her, is far from accurate today. She retains the intelligence and instincts she displayed at school and although she makes no pretence about her origins and will talk honestly and frankly – at times to her disadvantage, she has inevitably gained in social experience and sophistication since those early days in New York. In the mid-1960s there was a frenzy among young American women to follow the Streisand 'look'. As *Readers Digest*, reprinting from *Life* magazine, reported at the time: 'Hairdressers were besieged with requests for Streisand wigs [Beatle not kempt], and women's magazines hastily assembled features on the Streisand fashion [threadbare], and the Streisand eye make-up [proto-Cleopatra].' All that has long since gone of course, and her own attitudes have moderated over the years, though as she approaches fifty she is still disinclined to be a slave to fashion. She is said to dress simply and to please herself, yet is still capable of raising eyebrows when attending glittering show-business occasions.

The person likely to know Streisand best from those days when she was struggling to break into the business must surely be Elliott Gould. 'She was the most innocent thing I'd ever seen,' said Elliott recalling that time. 'But she was so strange that I was afraid.' Barbra's trip to California to do a television show brought about their first separation. She cried every day they were apart and once together again they decided to get married. Barbra's swift success changed their lifestyle dramatically and she switched in one frenzied move from a dowdy railroad flat to a luxury duplex penthouse twenty-one storeys above Manhattan. Though she lives for and in the present, she has always cherished the sentimental opportunities of life. When she and Elliott first met during the run of *I Can Get It For You Wholesale*, they swore never to be apart on their birthdays. On their first wedding anniversary Elliott gave her a white marble egg which she carried with her. Later she had playwright Isobel Lennart write the scene into *Funny Girl*.

Barbra is very much her own woman, a free spirit. As her career advanced she developed a keen sense of her own value, yet when working on something which is important to her emotionally as an individual – *Yentl* for instance – the project will instinctively take precedent over financial implications. Much of Barbra's 'down' image has come from her professional obsession with perfection. Seldom is she totally satisfied with a scene and will often insist on doing a couple more takes even when the director has assured her that they are totally unnecessary.

She has an intense Taurean will power when she has a mind to use it. Because of her fierce commitment to a project, she forms definite views and will fight hard on the set for anything she believes to be right. She is positive and single-minded in the extreme and will not hesitate to implant her views with force and conviction. This can take her into demarcated areas, aggravating personal relationships and bruising egos.

This also underlines the contradictions in her personality, because in her private life she has often shown herself to be shy, unsure and withdrawn. At times she has become virtually reclusive, such has been her antipathy towards outside influences. She believes, too, that her private life is her own affair and has never really come to terms with the insistent pressure of media attention. She is reluctant to acknowledge that, as one of the world's greatest entertainers, she has any kind of obligation to the public or the press, outside the commitment to work to the very extent of her energy and talent whenever she is performing. She always appears astonished that people should be interested in her for any reason other than for her status as a public performer and she repels with tigerish tenacity, any kind of intrusion into her private life. She can take the harshest criticism of her acting or singing with an easier grace.

No one is more individual. She makes up her own mind as she goes along, without thought of consistency or effect. She doesn't set out to be different, to make an impression or to gain attention. In these ways she is still extremely gauche. Nor would she conform to a predetermined lifestyle set by society as being appropriate to a Hollywood superstar. She has the ability to focus strongly on individual facets of life and, once she has decided, is fully committed. But that doesn't mean for life. She has an open mind and will not hesitate to alter her ideas or views. She wouldn't feel it necessary to give an explanation. So any comments she might have made at any time are not necessarily valid for life.

Perhaps one of the most accurate assessments of the complexities of Streisand was attributed to Barbra herself by *Associated Press* in July 1968: 'You really have to be yourself, no matter what. I have always wanted to excel in anything I tried ... I'm really a conglomorate of contradictions. But how can you appreciate the summer if you never had the winter?'

For someone who has become a goddess to millions, is recognized in scores of countries as 'the world's greatest female entertainer', has earned more than any other actress in history and is genuinely unique among entertainers, Barbra Streisand remains remarkably level-headed. She has her feet planted firmly on the ground. The no-nonsense postures she demonstrated as a skinny kid in the grey, drabness of 1940s Brooklyn, have remained with her as a steadying influence against the forces of excess ever present in the glamour and excitement of stardom.

The name she has made famous throughout the world is the one she was born with, save for the dropping of an 'a' and a second forename. It is easy to imagine it being essential to Barbra's philosophy for life which repels pretension, pomposity, fake and fabrication. Why use another name when her own is good enough? It comes within that part of her make-up which has resisted all persuasion to have her nose reshaped. There is the inherent drive to make it on her own, for the world to take her as she is. For Barbra it appears to be the ultimate challenge and is linked unequivocally with her enormous ego kindled during infancy when this puny youngster with the squinting eyes and large nose dared to have serious notions of becoming 'a star'. It is proof positive of her talent for anyone who doubted her ability to make it to the top and also, not least, to satisfy her inner self.

It seems she cast aside anything which would have made the going easier, like the nose job, pandering to popular taste, even voice coaching and the study of music. What you get from Streisand is pure Streisand – no artificial colourings, no quick-fixes. Though one of the greatest-ever stars in a fantasy world, Barbra knows well enough that beyond the footlights and outside the film and recording studio, the world is anything but fantasy. She once said: 'There's no such thing as wildest dreams coming true, especially if you're from Brooklyn. There you get a real beat on life, so you really have a sort of grasp of things as they are and there's no room for fantasy. You want the fantasy, but know it doesn't exist.'

Yet being a pragmatist doesn't make her any less of an individual and on many broad issues often she will have sectional opinions. Take her feminism, for instance. There is no doubt that her instincts react instantly to the merest hint of women being patronized, most particularly at a professional level, but her attitudes appear different from those articulated by recognized hard campaigners like Jane Fonda and Vanessa Redgrave. Her resistance makes her no less feminine and she likes being looked after and cosseted on dates.

'I don't know what my mother will say', said Barbra when told about
a possible nude scene in *The Owl and the Pussycat*

Bathtime with co-star George Segal in *The Owl and the Pussycat*, but there was no singing role for Barbra in the picture

Barbra turns blonde in the 1981-released movie *All Night Long*, with Gene Hackman. She reputedly received a 4-million dollar fee for her comparatively minor role as Cheryl Gibbons

A sick 'client' is hidden away while well-meaning callgirl/wife Barbra
diverts the attentions of husband Michael Sarrazin in the zany comedy
For Pete's Sake in 1974

In *Funny Lady*, Fanny Brice (Barbra) shows Billy Rose (James Caan)
just how to deliver his composition 'More Than You Know' at a
recording session

Meeting Queen Elizabeth II when *Funny Lady* was chosen for the British Royal Film Performance. Barbra travelled to London for the occasion. Seen in the line-up are Jon Peters (behind Barbra) and, alongside, James Caan, James Stewart and Lee Remick

Leaving Heathrow in November 1984 with her then boyfriend Richard Baskin, after shooting the Baskin-directed *Emotion* video in London

A Grammy for Barbra in 1977. She was the first entertainer to win all the major entertainment awards – an Oscar (cinema), Emmy (television), Tony (theatre) and Grammy (recording)

Song rehearsal for *Yentl* with lyricists Alan and Marilyn Bergman, and composer Michel Legrand. They received an Oscar in the Music (original score) category

Barbra discusses a forthcoming shot with Avigdor (Mandy Patinkin) and Hadass (Amy Irving). *Yentl* was a major box office success

Opposite *Yentl* was a fifteen-year crusade for Barbra. In the end, she directed, produced, co-wrote and starred in the picture, but did not receive an Oscar. Amy Irving (pictured) was nominated in the Best Supporting Actress category

Six o'clock on Thursday, 29 March 1984 at the Leicester Square Theatre in London, venue for the Royal European Premiere of *Yentl*. The Euro promotion also included visits to France, Germany, Italy and Holland.

One Voice, taken from Barbra's first full-length concert in fifteen years, was the recording highlight of 1987, with the video release of the famous televised special making a strong impact

Streisand in the 1990s: as Dr Susan Lowenstein with Nick Nolte as
Tom Wingo in her latest film *The Prince of Tides*

In 1986 in New York a proclamation from governor Mario M. Cuomo declaring May 1-7 'New York Women in Film Week' was presented to her at the opening ceremony in Manhatten. While ackowledging the honour paid to her through her selection to receive the declaration, chosen for her accomplishments as producer, director and performer, she was also honest enough to announce: 'It is our [women's] instinct to nurture, to create life, not destroy it. We must see that vision realized. I look forward to the day we are recognized for the quality of our film making and not just because we are women.' She also added, significantly: 'It is ironic that there is no need to have a week to honour men in film...'.

Her own brand of realism she applies to other fundamental issues of life. She believes in God, for instance, but whether she would claim to be religious in the orthodox sense is another matter. She once told *Ladies' Home Journal* that the Orthodox (Jewish) training is outdated, but she felt it to be wrong not to guide young people, adding that '... I think it's an unfair burden to teach them nothing, to say, "I don't know, decide for yourself".' She revealed her own deep thinking on such basic issues in the same interview. 'Science isn't everything,' she said. 'No one is going to come up with a scientific reason for dying. Organized religion is something I couldn't subscribe to, but it's important to have a sense of God, a sense of mystery.' This perhaps answers those critics who ask how she can believe in God yet retain her liberal views on partners outside marriage.

Her honesty, which often reveals itself to associates, the media and therefore the public, as a predilection to being outspoken and frank, is no more than the yardstick she applies to herself. She readily acknowledges the weaknesses in her own character, one of which is manifest in her own feelings of insecurity. In the early 1980s, when she had long since acquired a monumental reputation and matching success as an actress and singer and was considered to be one of the most charismatic celebrities of the day, she admitted that her fear of success was still worse then her fear of failure. And despite the public image of a strong, immovable Streisand knowing exactly what she is doing and where she is going, and insisting on everything being done to her formula, she told *Newsweek* in 1966: 'I have fifty ways to do everything. I love it when a director makes up my mind for me. I wish they would do it more often. I don't know why they don't. Maybe they're afraid.'

Once Barbra is into a project which captures her interest and imagination, her dedication is virtually limitless; and she admits that her ego is too big for her to be influenced by or jealous of other people. This latter aspect of her character is not always calculated to win friends and influence people, often sounding insufferably boastful, as when she was interviewed by the *Chicago Tribune* at the time of *Funny Girl* in 1964. Said Barbra: 'I don't want to imitate anybody. Besides, this show is fate. The play is really about me; it simply happened to happen before to Fanny Brice. And anyway, it's fictionalized.'

She possesses a 'voice in a million' yet never fully seems to appreciate the natural gift. She once told *Playboy* that she wished she could sing like Aretha Franklin. 'I'm inspired by talent,' she said. 'I love Lee Wiley, Ethel Waters, Billie Holiday.' Few would argue about her ability to work hard, both physically and mentally. Her natural reserves of both are remarkable; and there seems little remorse even when the outcome isn't as successful as it might have been.

Take *Hello Dolly!* for example. She told *Celebrity*: 'I searched for the parts of me that were right for Dolly and that's what I used. I have an instinct about a character and I try to be faithful to myself and to the character and to the moment. This is what is fun in films, because movies are a spontaneous medium. When there is a feeling of spontaneity, that's when the character really comes across.' For Streisand, the picture's commercial failing wasn't really the issue. When looking back on *Funny Girl* she said that she could remember every line of every script. 'I played forty two different scenes,' she revealed. 'The one I did opening night on Broadway was a new scene that day. We were doing the first scene of the movie and I remembered a great line Isobel [Lennart] had written. She'd even forgotten it, but we found it and we used it. It was perfect.'

Two features dominant in the life of Streisand which she has never completely comes to terms with are the nasty things the press say about her and the handling of her own success. America's Gene Shalit talked to her about the former in an exlusive television interview on *The Today Show* in November 1987. That she gave such an interview was remarkable enough, because of her natural distaste of such experiences, and she was there only to help plug her forthcoming picture, *Nuts*. Barbra, as ever, was outspoken: 'I cannot control what people say about me, what they write about me, what they invent about me because, you know, they can't get to talk to me because I don't like to give interviews. I'd rather my work speak for itself and that's the only thing I can control in some ways, is my work, and that's why I pay a lot of attention to it.'

Shalit seized the opportunity to probe deeper on this significant point, suggesting that Barbra was perhaps in a *Catch-22* situation. Responding to his earlier question on whether she wanted to be liked, she had said: 'Yeah, sure, why not?' so Shalit now suggested that a) she wanted to be liked; b) she does not give interviews; c) the press, knowing she won't give interviews, gets angry and therefore writes articles that makes people not like her. Barbra agreed. 'So why don't you talk to the press and get it over with?' asked Shalit. Barbra replied: 'Well, you know, I do and I have, but the last paper I gave an interview to was my friend's son's – a school newspaper. He's ten. I liked that one. But the thing is, I just can't bear the things taken out of context. I can't bear it and I don't know ... I've never gotten used to it. I've been in this business twenty-five years, Gene!' Then (smiling), 'I'm an old broad already, but I can't fathom somebody not telling the truth.'

Revealing, certainly, but one is still left with the feeling that it doesn't tell the whole story and that within Barbra there is an underlying nervousness and tension about the press. It probably comes from her natural inclination to have complete control over everything she does. She appreciates that problems arise through her attitude towards the media, yet somehow that seems preferable to hanging out the welcome sign, for then she would lose control completely and it would be even more difficult, for instance, to keep her private life to herself.

Shortly after her success with *Funny Girl*, she told the *Long Island Press*: 'I never intend to be difficult or hard to get. When I'm performing – I'm not afraid of anything or anybody. But when I'm just me, I have this fright of being a disappointment to people, reporters and yes, to fans. I can't shake the feeling that they're going to look at me and think, "What's so special about her"?'

Barbra certainly isn't very adept at handling her own success. One gets the feeling that she would far sooner be working quietly on a project, away from the media and the public, totally

Barbra Streisand

immersed in what she is doing with as much control as possible
over the way it is being advanced. Her ambitions at director and
producer level bear witness to this. Seldom can she be
persuaded to make personal appearances to promote her own
pictures. It is almost a paranoia that her work must stand or fall
on its merit – that her performance will in some way be debased
in her own mind if it has to depend on, or benefit from, the
impetus of personal promotion.

This attitude has to be admired in an artist when television
interview programmes and talk shows are dominated by movie
stars and show-biz people blatantly and cynically plugging their
latest endeavour. Streisand faces similar difficulties in giving
concerts and making personal professional appearances. For
many years now she would only have had to name her own
price, but steadfastly she resists all offers to bring her face to face
with her adoring public. On this point Barbra, as always, is
honest with herself. In 1982 she admitted to *Esquire* magazine
that she was not comfortable with her success: '... I never was. I
don't like being recognized. I don't know that I'm like a famous
person or star. I feel just like a workaholic. Sometimes when I
was around people like Sophia Loren or Elizabeth Taylor they
were like stars to me. They acted in a certain kind of way ...
they're very comfortable with the press, with photographers ... I
don't think I'll ever get used to it.'

No one can deny the dynamism of Barbra Streisand ... in the
movies, as a recording artist, giving a concert and as a private
individual. Notwithstanding the complicated nature of her
character, the way she picks and chooses her material, the long
gaps between films, the numerous untruths which have been
told and reported about her, few would deny that she remains
one of the most compelling, exciting, talented, dedicated and
charismatic celebrities in the world today.

She is also among the most admired by her show-business
contemporaries. Some time ago the fan magazine *All About
Barbra* solicited the views of a number of artists in a three-page
feature entitled 'The Singers' Singer. The views would give
pleasure to Barbra. Olivia Newton-John, who once tied with
Streisand as America's choice for favourite singer, said: 'I think
she is a phenomenon, one of the few who can seemingly do it
all.' Sheena Easton said that Barbra was her musical idol: 'I
always wanted to sound like her and I'd phrase songs the way

she did.' Lena Horne said 'There's only one Streisand' while
John Travolta said he got hooked on her voice. 'Once you've
heard Streisand do a song first, the next person you hear singing
it seems all wrong.'

Considering that Barbra Streisand's public persona is not
particularly 'consumer friendly', except of course among her
thousands of loyal fans, she should be able to take considerable
comfort from the high opinion almost universally expressed of
her impeccable professionalism. That corporate assessment
gains considerable substance when you consider that it has been
gained, not by pandering to media triviality, lowering her
standards to become more popular, or responding to continuing
pressure to be different, more acquiescent and obliging.

She has carved out her own star–audience relationship
without compromising her own ideals. As Richard Dyer in *The
Movie* so aptly put it: '... she is also assertive and thereby breaks
another set of rules, those of femininity. There always have been
strong independent women stars – Crawford, Davis, Hepburn,
Stanwyck are the classics – but they seldom challenged male
egos and were usually put into plots where at the end of the day
they had to climb down and sink into the arms of the leading
man. Streisand is not like this. Her insistent presence obliterates
the male stars' egos; and the plots of her films either show her
winning on her own terms as she does in *What's Up Doc?*, or
ending defiant in *Funny Girl*, plucky in *The Way We Were*, or
triumphant in *A Star Is Born*, if she loses her man.' The same
writer points out another dimension to her assertiveness, that
she must be the first star since Jolsen who has used Jewishness
not just for laughs, but for emotion and glamour as well.

As a link to discovering Barbra Streisand as a person, who
should know her better than the man who was once her lover
and business partner. Jon Peters seriously came into her life in
the mid-1970s and Barbra scandalized Hollywood by making the
one-time hairdresser the producer of her next movie, *A Star Is
Born*. Jon described her as powerful, gentle and beautiful; fun to
be with. 'She's ten different people,' he added. In Streisand's
withdrawal from the constant intensity of stardom there is also
possibly an element of self-preservation. Keeping the superstar
trappings at arms' length enables her to maintain a perspective
on life, to keep her in touch with reality. It protects her from
being consumed by the system. She once said: 'The pressures of

this business can destroy you, like they did Judy Garland. You have to be very strong to avoid it. The thing that keeps me sane is living here [her Malibu beach house]. It's away from it all. I don't hear traffic sounds. I don't answer the phone much on weekends. I garden or walk or ride my bike.'

Someone who should know Barbra Streisand better than anyone is Barbra herself. So how does she see herself? Who can tell, for the duality of her person means that although she is outgoing, vocal, excitable and at times lavish with her comments, she is also enigmatic and paradoxical. But maybe she was getting close to the real Barbra Streisand when she said in 1983: 'I was never comfortable being a star. Star is a kind of embarrassing word for me. Maybe that's why I get a lot of flak from the press. I never thought it was necessary to expose my personal life. I hope people enjoy my work – that's what they pay for – but I don't believe they have any claim on my personal life or my personal time. The thoughts and feelings I want to express, I do ... in my work.'

It may not tell us all we would like to know about Barbra Streisand, but the specification is about right: it is simply stated, honest, places the performer–audience relationship in the ingenuous juxtaposition she has always judged it to be, and suggests that she should stand or fall on the success or otherwise of her work. In her world, so far as anyone else is concerned, nothing more should matter.

8 *Greatest Female Entertainer in the World*

It is not surprising that where the chemistry with Streisand's co-stars had been right there were persistent calls for a re-match. After all, the ploy was not new to Hollywood. Once stars had been brought together successfully, a follow up was likely to provide a valuable head start at the box-office. Everyone waited impatiently for Barbra to work again with Robert Redford, but it wasn't to happen. The campaign for her to star once more with Ryan O'Neal was more successful ... though not for seven years did they feature together again in a motion picture. Individual commitments were often a problem when trying to stage a follow-up or sequel and by no means had Barbra been idle during the 1970s. Between 1974 and 1979 four new Streisand movies were to be released and she would consolidate and extend her reputation as a top recording artist. The occasional concert and high-profile television appearance would add to a full and committed lifestyle.

When the LP of *A Happening In Central Park* was released by Columbia in 1968 Streisand, though only twenty six, was already a veteran on record. Since signing her first recording contract with Columbia president Goddard Lieberson, she had brought out no fewer than twelve long-players in just five years. Together with some eighteen LPs which were to follow up to the mid-1970s, they would be a mixed bag, showcasing a collection of songs which, through her interpretation, would accurately reflect Streisand's own capricious talent. The *People* album, which Columbia brought out in 1964 as a follow-up to the *Funny*

119

Girl original cast recording (not to be confused with the soundtrack from the picture, which didn't show until 1968), created an enormous impact, largely because of the haunting Bob Merrill–Jule Styne title song which was to become an all-time Streisand classic. This beautifully constructed ballad was the perfect vehicle for Barbra's exciting, dramatic, yet shaded and responsive interpretation and the album secured Barbra her second Grammy as Best Female Vocalist. When the single was released it was an instant best-seller and the song became indelibly and almost exclusively associated with Streisand.

Such was her dominance of the musical scene at about this time that during one week in October 1964 her first four solo LPs, plus the *Funny Girl* original cast recording, were all at the same time in the top 100 in the United States. The *People* album was the first Streisand recording to top America's Billboard charts and the single was nominated for Record of the Year and Song of the Year.

Some albums, like *My Name Is Barbra* (1965) and *Color Me Barbra*, a year later, were taken from her television specials. Here again she made her own rules, for CBS-TV saw so much potential in Streisand that on the strength of a few guest appearances they not only signed her up for her own show, but gave her extraordinary freedom with its presentation. It was typical of Barbra that she ignored the usual format of guest stars and gave what was virtually a one-woman show. It was a gamble which some might have seen as arrogance, but Barbra's courage paid off and before a viewing audience of some 50 million she became an overnight television sensation. The show was to collect five Emmy Awards, including Streisand's own Outstanding Individual Achievement in Entertainment award. Two separate albums were put out at different times by Columbia covering the television special and both consolidated Barbra's success, each reaching number two in the Billboard charts with the second LP doing better by remaining in the charts for almost fifty weeks.

Sticking with a successful formula, Barbra followed the basic format for *Color Me Barbra*, which was televised in March 1966. This time there were reports of tensions and frustrations during the tapings with Streisand's temperament and impatience showing from the emotional strain, but nothing could stop the

Streisand bandwagon and her latest television offering, when transmitted, was acclaimed with even more enthusiasm than the first and received another five Emmy Awards. An album put out under the *Color Me Barbra* title was wide-ranging, and included an absorbing medley of thirteen songs, many linked not surprisingly to the theme of 'face'. Some of these are Streisand at her very best, the exceptional voice soaring magnificently to top register, yet still restrained, in 'Funny Face', and there is a spine-tingling version of 'I've Grown Accustomed to Her Face' – an all-too-brief snatch unfortunately, but sensitively executed.

Probably the best of the medley is left until the end when Barbra showcases not only her unquestionable range and technique, but also her sensitivity and individuality in changing just the occasional note here and there, and providing a memorable finale with those haunting and natural Streisand melodies, 'I Stayed Too Long at the Fair' and 'Look at That Face'.

The album also includes 'One Kiss', 'The Minute Waltz', 'Gotta Move', 'Non C'est Rien', 'Where or When', 'Where Am I Going?' and 'Starting Here, Starting Now'. But worthy of special attention is a down-tempo version of 'C'est Si Bon' which for the majority of Streisand fans must be the most stylish and individual interpretation of this popular song ever recorded. She captivates listeners instantly with an incredibly high yet sweetly ringing and tuneful note in the opening phrase and is later creative and courageous enough to surprise and almost shock with a couple of spine-chilling flattened notes which are as exciting as they are unexpected. The whole thing is beautifully scored and if her uneasy improvisation once or twice is trite enough almost to threaten the performance, her handling of this lovely melody including its ending on a defiantly held minor note, is breathtaking, different, exquisite and matchless. The album, when compared with the more mature Streisand voice of the 1980s, occasionally provides a singularly apt example of a more youthful Barbra, fresh and adventurous with an inimitable interpretive talent.

Judging the punters' mood is not easy, even for Streisand, and after two rocketing television successes, Barbra's third presentation called *The Belle of Fourteenth Street* failed to the extent that Columbia's plans to release an album of the show were abandoned. In an effort to anticipate public needs Marty

Erlichman, who had been executive producer on the two earlier successes, considered a change of format necessary and the final presentation, giving rather less of unadulterated Barbra, paid the price of changing a winning formula with considerably reduced ratings.

The 1960s had seen Streisand developing as an interpreter of broadly based musical standards mingled with a core of soundtrack albums from her own shows, including *Funny Girl* of course, *Hello Dolly!*, put out by 20th Century Fox Records in 1969, and *On a Clear Day You Can See Forever* and *The Owl and the Pussycat*, released by Columbia in 1971. But by this time Barbra was being urged to look to the future, to become more contemporary and respond to change as rock left its obscure beginnings behind and crossed over into the mainstream of popular music. In a sense it was the only way for Barbra to go. She had never demonstrated a capacity for, nor a real inclination towards, becoming an out-and-out swinging singer of standards. Her sense of rhythm is not great and despite her exceptional vocal range, purity of tone and genuinely unique sound, her phrasing isn't her best feature. With versatility a powerful force for Streisand the singer as well as for Streisand the actress, Barbra towards the end of the 1960s made a conscious transition into the contemporary sounds of the day.

What About Today provided the first opportunity for album collectors to hear the new Streisand. Released to the public in 1969, it was followed by *Stoney End* in early 1971 and *Barbra Joan Streisand* later that same year. The first album took her comfortably into this transitional stage, even accepting the stiltiness and lack of relaxation on some of the tracks. There was also the hint of a reluctance completely to foresake the past, with everyone involved including Streisand content to play it safe. The choice of material seems to confirm this and indeed, it was her outstanding singing of the Bacharach–David classic 'Alfie', hardly a contemporary offering inspired by the rock revolution, which shone out brilliantly from the remainder of the material, which includes some Streisand humour in 'With a Little Help From My Friends', and other predictable pieces like 'What About Today' and 'The Morning After'.

Stoney End was better and probably the best she was to produce during this period, though some would give good marks to *Barbra Joan Streisand* which followed; but it didn't rate highly with some critics. With a collection of material which was to demonstrate the finesse she could now produce on recordings, Barbra took her lead from some of the top names of the day on *Stoney End*, including Randy Newman, Gordon Lightfoot and Harry Nilsson. She is less theatrical, more spontaneous and delivers with a directness, clarity and conviction which was not replicated in the later album. Barbra is probably at her best with 'Just a Little Lovin' ', at her most adventurous, though perhaps unhappily self-conscious and forced, with the gospel-type version with chorus of Lightfoot's 'If You Could Read My Mind', and at her most successful in a rhythmic interpretation of the title song, the single becoming one of her biggest successes.

The third offering, *Barbra Joan Streisand*, has well-chosen material from an array of top composers of the day and Barbra sometimes has to struggle to meet the demands of such a broad musical canvas, which included Joe Cocker, Carole King and John Lennon. Confident and assured, she is also at times stylish and exciting, but surely fitting more comfortably into the mode of Bacharach and David than some of the others. Stephen Holden was plain enough when he told *Rolling Stone* readers, as pointed out by Donald Zec and Anthony Fowles: 'An unqualified bummer is Barbra's rendition of John Lennon's "Mother" in which she belts out the primal scream. A mechanized shriek that has all the humanity of a police siren, it makes an embarrassing mockery of a great song.' But as Holden also pointed out, the Bacharach–David medley was pure vintage Streisand ... the ultimate in pop professionalism and he went so far as to suggest that perhaps she and not Dionne Warwick would seem to be the singer best suited to record the complete Burt Bacharach–Hal David songbook. But as for the Carole King or John Lennon songbooks, concludes Holden, 'God forbid!'

Barbra probably scores best of all with 'A House Is Not a Home' and 'One Less Bell to Answer', for which she had first received critical acclaim on the *Burt Bacharach TV Special* a short time before, and with an impeccable interpretation of Michel Legrand's 'The Summer Knows'. Streisand enthusiast, the late Dennis M. Pallante, told readers of *All About Barbra* that her voice was reaching its peak at about this time. 'Never again would her voice be as rich and full as it is on some of the best cuts,' he judged. Some later material, none the less, would bring her greater commercial success. The *A Star Is Born* album, for instance, reached a phenomenal sale in excess of 5 million. However, *Barbra Joan Streisand* reached a commendable number eleven on the Billboard chart and within four months had achieved Gold status in America.

It was also in 1971 that Streisand, as part of the essential process of updating her image, agreed to a rare guest appearance on television, appearing on the *Burt Bacharach Special* along with Rudolf Nureyev and Tom Jones. She had virtually shunned this most-powerful-of-all media since the early days of her career so her appearance was a major event, and not just for her fans. She didn't let anyone down. Wearing little make-up and with long blonde hair falling about her shoulders she looked particularly stunning and chatted amiably and comfortably with Bacharach, telling him that while she still loved the old songs, it was time for her to move into the present. Then came the inspired sequence when, through double-camera exposure, Barbra sings a duet with herself. Altogether she gives a most inspired visual and vocal performance, mixing intensity with restraint, projection with unpretentiousness and abandonment with moderation.

Appearing on the *Burt Bacharach TV Special* was a wise career move for Barbra at that time. She looked smooth and sexy in a natural way, was seductive without being over-coy, her conversations with her host were fresh and easy and included a captivating hint of self-effacement; her clothes sense was impeccable. This was superstar Streisand at her best and there is little doubt that, largely resulting from her contribution to the presentation, Burt Bacharach received an Emmy for the show. It is interesting, too, that although the *Special* gives the impression of being performed before a live audience, the audience applause track was added afterwards, for Barbra was already developing her phobia about live audiences. It is hard to pin-point how this came about, but that it exists there can hardly be any doubt. In some thirty years of recording she put out only three 'live' albums, and for a performer of such dynamism and presence, that is astonishing. Barbra herself probably would be hard-pressed to put forward a convincing reason for her antipathy towards appearing live. It seems to be instinctive and has little to do with logic. It could be linked to her obsession with perfection in all she does. That is why she likes movie making best of all, followed by recording. In both these areas you can go over things time and again, polishing them up and smoothing them out, and once it is right it can be locked in for all time, for posterity. With a live performance you're stuck with what you have been able to produce at the time – no going back, no chance to make it just that little better.

It must be one of the major disappointments of Barbra's career, for everyone except Barbra herself, that is, that the opportunity for her fans to see her live have been so limited, particularly when she is such an exciting and atmospheric performer. When prised out into the open again in April 1972 to sing before 18,000 at the Forum in Los Angeles in support of Senator George McGovern's presidential campaign, it was her first public concert since her concert in Central Park, New York, in the summer of 1967. And her next full-length concert to be recorded live, wasn't for almost another fifteen years.

The Forum concert, unlike the earlier Central Park offering, took place at an indoor venue and the recording which became available therefore is of superior quality, with an audience in size and temperament which, unlike Central Park (too large and distilled) and the Malibu concert which was to come much later (too exclusive), provided the opportunity for a closer rapport with her audience. Despite the earlier billing of such luminaries as James Taylor, Carole King and Quincy Jones, Streisand was the magical attraction and responded with a performance which one commentator described as ecstatic and others consented was vivid, thrilling and professional. Familiarity helped to keep her in-born fear of a live audience under control, for she came to the Forum only a few months after her cabaret success at the Hilton in Las Vegas. Most of the Streisand specials featured there were included in her outstanding performance at the Forum with 'Don't Rain On My Parade' and 'Starting Here, Starting Now' picked out by many observers as show-stoppers.

It wasn't until 6 September 1986 that she got together with Barry Gibb at her Malibu home and estate in California for her next major live concert, inspired once again by her political leanings towards the Democratic Party, and in particular, as an expression of her deep anxieties over America's nuclear policy following the disaster at Chernobyl. She had admitted earlier that she could never have imagined herself wanting to sing in public again, and for weeks before had worried about the performance, sleeping badly and suffering panic palpitations.

And after welcoming her guests, who were there at $2,500 apiece, she said: 'My fear of the world situation is greater than my fear of performing. I could no longer remain silent. By my silence I was giving consent to the madness of nations.' This special gala presentation, called 'One Voice', spanned the whole of Barbra's career, and included such Streisand standards as 'People', 'Evergreen', 'Somewhere' and 'Happy Days Are Here Again'. She did two duets with Barry Gibb, 'What Kind of Fool?' and 'Guilty', both from the highly successful recording session she did with Gibb, and produced by him, in 1980. There was 'Papa, Can You Hear Me?' from *Yentl*, and a courageous tribute to Judy Garland with her singing of 'Over the Rainbow'. The show produced glowing reports and altogether brought in more than $5 million for the cause.

Obviously this was not an occasion for the average punter, although record and tape versions of 'One Voice' were widely bought by Streisand fans. Back in the mid-1970s, however, with Barbra well distanced from full-blown concert performances, they could enjoy her occasional appearances on television, buy a generous output of recordings, and pay to see her at the cinema box-office in four more feature movies before the end of the decade, the first being released in 1974.

In *For Pete's Sake*, she co-starred with Michael Sarrazin, who in 1969 had appeared with Jane Fonda in a story of the dance marathons of the Depression, *They Shoot Horses, Don't They?* His pairing with Streisand in a comedy intended to build on the success of *The Way We Were*, is pleasant enough without breaking through any new barriers, and the film itself is reasonable entertainment and enjoyable. Produced by Marty Erlichman – it was his first effort, and Stanley Shapiro, and directed by Britain's Peter Yates, known for *Bullitt*, the picture was fashioned as a screwball comedy to match the earlier *What's Up Doc?*, but by general concensus, it never quite made it.

Sarrazin is Pete and Barbra is Henrietta Robbins, a young Brooklyn couple who want a better lifestyle. The idea is for Pete to give up his taxi-driving so he can go back to full-time study at college and, on a tip-off to invest in the stockmarket, Henri borrows $3,000 on the strength of the investment, to cover Pete's further education. But it takes time for the investment to pay off so Henri agrees to sell off her debt by working for a local madame, at the same time considering her prostitution excusable since she is doing it to help secure the future for her husband and herself.

It is an hilarious episode when one of her clients, a judge, suffers a heart attack in her closet and attempts are made to hide him away as her husband, unaware of her secret activities, arrives home. The incidents become zanier as her 'contract' is sold to a couple of so-called businessmen and then to cattle thieves, Barbra in a blonde wig becoming entangled with the law, a package which includes a bomb, and finally an elaborate cattle chase.

The story was specially written by co-producer Stanley Shapiro and Maurice Richlin for a Marty Erlichman project specially constructed for Streisand. It appears that the problem was that with Barbra being virtually the only female superstar at that time, there was a notable absence of 'off-the-peg' material suitable for her. Even if the concept of the film seemed strange, and few would class it among Barbra's best offerings, reviews overall were surprisingly good and it did extraordinarily well at the box-office. It probably suffered by appearing lightweight after her deeper performances in *Up the Sandbox* and *The Way We Were*, and through being labelled more as time went on as the film which led to her meeting and subsequent romance with Jon Peters, diverting some of the attention from the movie itself.

The short hairstyle which Barbra wore held the key to their liaison. Peter Yates wanted a new style to give her a completely fresh look, but she was reluctant to have her own hair cut and restyled. Later at a party she saw a style which she liked and discovered it had been done by Jon Peters, a fashionable Beverly Hills hairdresser. He was called in to design a close-cut wig specially for Barbra to wear in *For Pete's Sake*. Although Barbra would sing the title song to be heard over the titles, *For Pete's Sake* was yet another non-musical movie. Already those of her fans who wanted to see her again in a full-blooded singing role had waited four long years, but they didn't have to wait much longer, for by the time *For Pete's Sake* was released in June 1974, Barbra was already busy on her next picture, the long-awaited follow up to *Funny Girl*.

No thanks to Barbra. She didn't want to do *Funny Lady* because she felt it would be going back rather than looking forward and also, by this time, she had Jon Peters close at hand.

He didn't want her to do it either. It is quite likely that by this time both were more concerned to do a movie together where they could between them have a greater degree of control over the whole project. But *Funny Lady* was tempting to Barbra in one respect: it would complete her contractual obligations to Ray Stark, henceforth being a free agent. In finally agreeing to do the picture, Streisand consoled herself in believing that the two films would be very different. She accepted that there was a lot of Streisand in *Funny Girl*, whereas in *Funny Lady*, which concentrated on a maturer Fanny Brice, she would have more opportunity to portray a real character. It had taken Ray Stark some seven years to produce a sequel to his original production of the Fanny Brice story, but in the end, the waiting was worthwhile.

The story picks up where *Funny Girl* left off, concentrating on the relationship between Fanny Brice and Billy Rose, after Nicky Arnstein has divorced her. James Caan, who had become a major star after being featured as a promising newcomer in *The Godfather* in 1972, was cast as the streetwise Rose while Omar Sharif took over once more as Arnstein. Stark brought in Herbert Ross to direct the picture, as he had done *Pussycat*, and Peter Matz, associated with Barbra on many of her best-selling albums, was conductor–arranger.

The plot is reasonably predictable, but how close it is to reality is anyone's guess. Perhaps it doesn't matter anyway. Showman hustler Rose persuades Fanny to appear in a show he is putting together called *The Crazy Quilt*, but he doesn't know enough about it and has catastrophically over-produced the show. He persuades Fanny to put it right and she reshapes it into a big hit. As it begins a highly successful Broadway run, Fanny sees Nick Arnstein in the audience and when he goes round to her dressing room after the show she tells him she still loves him. But as she kisses his hand she sees he is wearing a wedding ring and discovers that he has married an older woman for her money.

After a while Rose asks Fanny to marry him and she accepts. Things are all right for a time, but as Fanny continues to be a big star and Billy Rose becomes absorbed with rehearsals for his new show, they spend a lot of time apart. Fanny becomes disillusioned and is drawn once more to her old love for Arnstein. She tells Rose she must see Arnstein again, but when she does she rejects his idea that they could get together again, despite his being married, seeing him for the rogue he always was. She returns to Rose, but finds him in bed with the star of his new show. Fanny and Rose agree to a divorce, but some years later meet again when he tells Fanny that his new love was only after his money. It is obvious that they have an affection for each other, but when he asks her to star in his latest show, she doesn't give him a direct answer, saying only that she will think about it.

Making the picture had its problems. Barbra admitted that having Jon Peters on the set was a distraction which, according to Herb Ross, meant that she really didn't appear all that interested in doing the picture. Years later, in an exclusive preview of the film's video release, Steve Whicker in *All About Barbra* blamed director Herbert Ross for failing to grasp what William Wyler had earlier realized with *Funny Girl*: that the public was expecting to see and hear the Barbra Streisand they had come to know. Says Whicker: 'Ross misses that vital point completely to the extent that in *Funny Lady* several of Barbra's songs [some of the best performances in the film] are cut short ['More Than You Know'] or are obscured by dialogue as they start ['Great Day'] or before they finish ['If I Love Again'], and the audience is left struggling to hear Barbra's voice or suffering the frustration of hearing only half of her performance. It's an error of judgement which should have been noticed and corrected before the film was released.'

There is little doubt that the success of *Funny Lady* is due to a performance of strength and conviction from Barbra. Her portrayal of the older Fanny Brice struggling to balance the conflicting emotional enticements of Billy Rose, her career and Nicky Arnstein, is a joy. It is an example of perfect, if obvious casting, for no one could have played the part better. Streisand's lengthy connection with, and deep study of, Fanny Brice, her life and times, through her Broadway and West End success and then the movie, placed her in a unique position to handle the role.

A more surprising success was James Caan. At first an unlikely choice for the part of Billy Rose, his performance showed an intelligent and sensitive appreciation of what was required.

Not all reviews of *Funny Lady* were favourable, however,

perhaps emphasizing the difficulties which always accompany a film sequel. Critics marked down the unflattering costumes made for Barbra, even if they were authentic to the period, an emasculated script, and there was some general disappointment over the musical content, much of which was made up of existing material, though Streisand's singing was well up to standard. 'More Than You Know' was taken at a slow tempo and beautifully handled by Barbra; and her slower, measured singing of 'Great Day' (where her stunning costume incidentally, is extremely flattering), before she disappointingly breaks into a faster, more frantic up-tempo delivery, must surely be one of the most spine-tingling versions of this musical standard ever produced. She also scores heavily with 'Me and My Shadow', 'Isn't This Better' and a lively version of 'How Lucky Can You Get' in a picture whose musical numbers also include 'Clap Hands Here Comes Charlie', 'Let's Hear It For Me' and 'It's Only a Paper Moon'.

There was a good deal of fuss later when Billy Rose's former wife Eleanor Holm, who had been married to him for fourteen years, claimed the picture stretched the truth about their relationship to the extent that much of it was nonsense. Seldom does a bio-pic escape such criticism, *Funny Lady* probably no more than many others. But for Barbra it meant the end of her original contract with Ray Stark. That for her was an enormous relief, but no matter how tedious and strained the commitment might have become over the years, there could be no denying that it had been extraordinarily successful. Their last film together consolidated Barbra's position as Hollywood's number-one female star, a status which undeniably owed much to her professional relationship with Ray Stark.

The picture premièred on 9 March 1975 in Washington DC at a charity concert arranged by Stark to benefit the Special Olympics, which the Kennedy family run each year for handicapped children. To support the good cause, Barbra had somehow managed to overcome her natural resistance to public performances and was reportedly annoyed when she discovered, too late, that Stark had built into the occasion a strong promotional content for *Funny Lady*.

Film clips from both *Funny Girl* and *Funny Lady* opened the proceedings, with many particularly interesting behind-the-scenes shots being included. A somewhat stilted chat between

Streisand and Caan with taped sections of the Special Olympics followed, before the concert was introduced by Dick Cavett. A standing ovation greeted Barbra as the curtain rose to show her at the top of a staircase with a full orchestra behind her. 'The Way We Were' was followed by 'Don't Rain On My Parade' and then came 'My Man' before Barbra was joined by Caan for 'It's Only a Paper Moon' and 'I Like Her'. Streisand just occasionally showed her nervousness, but mostly she sang beautifully and despite there having been little time for rehearsal, the show was a popular success. That same month the original soundtrack recording of *Funny Lady* was released through Arista Records in America, arranged and conducted by Peter Matz.

For many years Barbra could have named her own price for a television series, or could have spent most of her time giving concerts or guesting on shows, but she kept resolutely remote. Her fifth television special – *Barbra Streisand … and Other Musical Instruments* – would be broadcast in America on 2 November 1973, just a week after the release of her film, *The Way We Were*, but during the 1980s, even her film productivity would seriously decline, only three pictures being released then, compared with the nine which came out in the 1970s. Meanwhile … *Other Musical Instruments* would show a changing Streisand, more controlled and relaxed, and in the second half of the 1980s there would be two further Streisand movies and eight more albums.

The TV special brought a mixed critical response. Some of the numbers are delivered with a warmth and sensitivity; others are crudely over-produced. While a number of relatively obscure songs add variety, Barbra would arguably continue to sound best with material which has become associated with her. Her rendition of 'On a Clear Day' shows Barbra at her very best and holds a magic all its own. Columbia taped the special at their UK studios at Elstree, reviews were mostly favourable, and the show secured good ratings. CBS estimated that some 40 million Americans saw the programme, and it would win five Emmy awards.

The *Funny Lady* LP was preceded by *Butterfly*, which was released in October 1974, and followed by *Lazy Afternoon*, which came out in October 1975. The former was produced by Jon Peters and took some six months to complete at an astounding cost of $150,000. James Kimbrell in *Barbra, An Actress Who Sings*, suggests that Peters first got involved when Barbra simply asked him to come along when she was recording the LP, but then she asked him to design the cover. It seems that it would be Peters himself who would suggest he took over as producer of the recording session after the earlier producer, Al Schmitt, was fired by Streisand because she did not like the finished product. The result certainly showed Peters' influence, notwithstanding his sketchy musical experience.

The contemporary Streisand sang rock numbers and reggae along with rhythm and blues and the result was markedly different, a world away from the selection of standards which Barbra had originally intended to record. There was later reportedly some verbal rough and tumble between Streisand and Schmitt, but throughout it all the record did very well, reaching number thirteen in the American charts and gaining a gold distinction.

Lazy Afternoon, which followed *Butterfly*, was a much more familiar Streisand with Rupert Holmes, the album's co-producer (with Jeffrey Lesser), arranger and conductor, bringing her back to the more lilting sounds and closer to the style which earlier had made her such an exciting and thrilling talent. The LP also held a couple of pointers to the future. Barbra enjoyed the experience of working with Holmes so much that he would jump at the chance to work with her again within a few months on what would become commercially her most successful film, and one of the songs included on the *Lazy Afternoon* pressing was 'I Never Had It So Good' by Paul Williams and Ron Nichols. It was with the said Paul Williams that she was destined to share her second Oscar through their joint composition, *Evergreen*, from the same record-breaking picture.

Lazy Afternoon also included Stevie Wonder's 'You and I' and from Alan and Marilyn Bergman, Barbra's favourite lyricists, and composer Dave Grusin, there was 'A Child Is Born'. The remainder of the album consisted of, in addition to the well-known title song, 'My Father's Song', 'By the Way', the Four Tops number 'Shake Me, Wake Me', 'I Never Had It So Good', the Paul Williams–Roger Nichols number, 'Letters That Cross in the Mail', 'You and I', 'Moanin' Low' and the album's finale, 'Windscreen', which had been included on Rupert Holmes' first album.

During the remainder of the 1970s there would be seven more Streisand albums, two of which were taken from the original soundtrack of her movies *A Star Is Born*, released in November 1976, and *The Main Event* (June 1979). After *Lazy Afternoon* came *Classical Barbra*, on which she featured with the Columbia Symphony Orchestra. This was a complete diversion for Barbra and, while it was never intended to have a wide appeal, the LP was pleasant enough. Barbra, though vocally under-extended, handled some of the more popular output from composers like Handel, Schumann and Debussy, well enough, though it is not hard to understand why, in retrospect, Columbia delayed the project, being doubtful about its commercial prospects.

Streisand Superman, which followed *Classical Barbra*, was produced by Gary Klein who later remarked on the phenomenal lengths to which Barbra would go in reaching for perfection, at one time working through until 4 a.m. It was an effort well rewarded because the album made an instant impact, reaching number two on the Billboard chart and achieving 'Gold' in just two weeks. It became the fastest-selling album of her career, proving just how popular Streisand continued to be when singing lilting, middle-of-the-road numbers taken from the more conventional pop and rhythm listings.

Klein produced Barbra's next album, which capitalized on the success of the earlier formula with Streisand in excellent voice on a number of easily identified modern popular and show standards. Titled *Songbird*, it included the well-loved 'Tomorrow' from Annie and Neil Diamond's 'You Don't Bring Me Flowers'. The title song did well in Billboard's pop singles chart and the album soared ahead to become a double-platinum seller.

After producing *A Star Is Born*, Jon Peters quickly set to work on a somewhat off-beat suspense film called *Eyes of Laura Mars* and Streisand, who was not featured in the movie, can be heard on the original soundtrack album put out in July 1978, singing 'Prisoner', which was the theme from the movie. Four months later came Barbra Streisand's *Greatest Hits, Volume 2*, and then, after the soundtrack album of *The Main Event*, her last album to be released in the 1970s, called *Wet*, became available in October 1979. Once more produced by Gary Klein, *Wet* was a concept album based on the theme of the title and was a carefully chosen selection of melodic songs from 'Come Rain or Come Shine', by those miracle men of traditional standards, Johnny Mercer and Harold Arlen, to 'No More Tears (Enough is Enough)', a rousing disco offering in which she broke new ground by singing duet with Donna Summer. This track just had to be included in the album for as a single released a short time ahead of the album it was to sell over a million copies.

Bringing the two singers together was an inspirational move for, as James Kimbrell put it: 'Elegant, energetic belting from Streisand and the lusty disco phrasing from Summer created a super-hit single, that was characterized as the major musical motif of the decade – chic sexuality with a dance beat.' He added that doubling on the duet gave Streisand the association with a hot record seller and gave Summer the prestige of teaming with a pop legend.

Barbra Streisand had come a long way during the 1970s. In particular her rating as a recording artist soared as she extended her influence on a broad front. She showed with consummate style her ability to handle show numbers, pop, rock, ballads, standards, rhythm and blues; even soul and the popular classics. The range was exceptional and she had the ability and charisma to attract her own core following in each category as well as maintaining her mainstream reputation. She approached the 1980s as one of the leading singers of the decade. Her duet with Neil Diamond on 'You Don't Bring Me Flowers' became her biggest-selling single and took just four weeks to claim the number-one slot across America.

But in movie-making terms, the 1970s were by no means over for Barbra. *A Star Is Born*, released in 1976, would pitch most critics into a state of apoplexy, yet the picture smashed box-office records, would become the ninth most successful film ever made, and gross something approaching $100 million. For *The Main Event*, released by Warner Brothers in 1979, Barbra would at last satisfy her clamouring fans by teaming once more with glamour star Ryan O'Neal. And among a whole catalogue of awards and distinctions the readers of *Photoplay Magazine* voted her their favourite motion picture actress for the second year in succession.

9 Never Mind the Critics

The influences which came together in Streisand's rock remake of *A Star Is Born* were powerful elements in themselves. Collectively they were potentially of powder-keg proportions. By this time Barbra and Jon Peters were deeply attracted to each other and the sum of the whole was infinitely more devastating than the individual parts. Peters was not the sort to placidly observe events. Nor was he inhibited by his lack of experience in the movie-making business. He had made his way in the world by pushing hard for what he wanted and had become a clever and successful 'street fighter' long before his time.

Born to an Italian mother and a Cherokee Indian father in one of the roughest parts of California, he was finished with school at twelve, ran away from home, and was a fourteen-year-old looking for work in New York in 1959. He had already spent time at a reform school. He talked himself into a job at a twenty-four-hour hairdressing salon and began to learn the business. He dropped the 'h' from his name and moved from one salon to another, in his element among so many females charmed by his glib, flattering line of patter.

At twenty-one he returned to California to open his own salon. At twenty-six he was the owner of four salons and a self-claimed millionaire. Good-looking and glamorous, he pulled some of the richest and most famous clients into his salon in Rodeo Drive in expensive Beverly Hills. The satirical and sexy picture *Shampoo*, in 1975, was cynically alleged by some critics, though inaccurately, to be based on Peters. Supposedly married as an early teenager, he later married actress Lesley Ann Warren, but at the time of *A Star Is Born*, his liaison with

Streisand was all that was exciting, passionate and glamorous in his love life. They made a compelling, formidable pair.

Adding to the highly charged personalities of Streisand and Peters under the auspices of *A Star Is Born*, was Kris Kristofferson, whose reputation as a drinker at the time was every bit a match for his fame as an entertainer. He was recruited to be Barbra's co-star. Meanwhile, the clear-minded, forthright and highly regarded Frank Pierson, who insisted on being allowed to direct the movie before agreeing to do the necessary rewrites to the script (though he had directed only one previous movie), added to the potentially explosive atmosphere as everyone began to assemble on the set.

When filming began in early 1976 this new version of *A Star Is Born* had already become notorious. For a start, the idea had been stuck on the launch-pad for several years and Barbra had turned it down more than once. It was Jon's idea for her to play the part ... he believed in it, she said later. When it did emerge as a runner under the banner of Barbra's own company, First Artists, there was an immediate bust-up, with Kristofferson reportedly set to walk out of the project because his name was planned to appear below the title, though much later he denied this was the case. Some critics were fanfaring the picture as a monumental Streisand–Peters egomaniacal indulgence as the jostling over who does what ended with Barbra as executive producer, Jon as producer, Kristofferson as co-star, Pierson as scriptwriter and director, but with Streisand as collaborator, and Rupert Holmes as musical director, with additional songs from Paul Williams and Kenny Archer.

Clashes were inevitable with such highly charismatic individuals and at times the making of the picture was almost as turbulent as the scenario of the film itself. Rupert Holmes was to disappear as musical director and Kris Kristofferson's 'opening hours' lengthened as shooting progressed. Jon Peters, who with Barbra had earlier reportedly seen off four writers, three producers and two directors, was enthusiastically prone to extend his influence and authority over all aspects of the filming, as indeed was Barbra, and Pierson was soon complaining about Barbra's interference.

She later would criticize Pierson for his meekness and for not providing the decision and direction the picture and the cast required of him. Moreover, she clearly stated that the director was there to carry out her ideas. With so much personal control over a picture budgeted at around $6 million, Streisand herself oscillated disturbingly between extremes of mood – ecstatic and highly charged one time, lugubrious and negative another.

Barbra must have questioned more than once her decision to go ahead with the movie, after earlier turning down the part. The word going around at the time was that she was infatuated with Peters and he had wanted her to do the exciting, upbeat rock-and-pop version he had in mind as a means of contemporizing her image. Under his influence and persuasion she had eagerly agreed. The story of the picture was not new to Hollywood. It had been told twice before, even if you discount *What Price Hollywood?* in 1931, which was a somewhat different story with positive similarities. Janet Gaynor and Frederic March starred in the recognized first version in 1937, but a remake in 1953 with Judy Garland and James Mason co-starring became an enormous hit and the standard by which Streisand's latest version would be judged.

The challenge she and Peters faced was daunting. Judy had been compelling in the earlier picture, the style and intensity of her performance gaining from the way the screenplay, with all its pathos and human desperation, reflected Garland's own tragic circumstances. It had become acknowledged as her greatest-ever performance, enhanced by a truly memorable score which included 'The Man That Got Away' and 'Born In a Trunk'.

The story is simple and effective, and features the show-business mentor/starlet see-saw relationship of success and failure. Judy, as Esther Blodgett trying to make her way in show business as a singer, is seen and initially ridiculed by the drunken Norman Maine, an idolized film star. He none the less is captivated by her and later recognizes her talent, persuading her to take a screen test. It is successful, she is renamed Vicki Lester, and becomes a great star. She and Maine get married as her career begins to take off, but as his career starts to slide his drinking increases. He sinks further into depression and an alcoholic stupor as his career nose-dives, while Vicki enjoys increasing acclaim as a great star. Lost and dejected, relegated to taking telephone messages for his famous wife, he can stand it no longer. Turning up drunk at an Oscar ceremony he cringingly humiliates her in front of a distinguished audience by asking for a job. He agrees to go for medical treatment, ends up in court; but finally, in total despair, he walks out into the sea early one morning and drowns himself.

The celebrated George Cukor directed the Garland film and did not conceal his disappointment at not being invited to direct Streisand's contemporary version. Nor did those other critics who, after seeing the finished 1976 version, judged the picture to be pretentious, overbearing and arrogant. Casting the movie hadn't been easy and before Kristofferson, Presley reportedly had been considered for the co-starring role. Barbra, it seems, had supported the idea, but the timing wasn't right. The ex-Beatle Ringo Starr was also at one time a contender and there were reports that Britain's Elton John might be found a place. The suggestion was also put about that Jon Peters might take the male lead himself, but that could have been a cynical reaction to what many considered to be an overbearing degree of control of the movie being discharged by Streisand and her man. Barbra said later that there had been no thought of Jon playing in the film.

The Streisand film was altogether tougher, more rugged, and added a drugs element. It was more dramatic, an all-action musical epic, with a bolder, more outspoken script. It was a powerful portrait with a different, fiercely candid type of sensitivity between the two principal characters with less traditional sentimentality. While all these differences were to be enumerated by many observers as a basis for their preference for the earlier film, it should be remembered that there was, after all, more than twenty years between the two pictures and Streisand's *Star* probably captured the mood of the times as convincingly as Garland's had done. To that extent it was unfair to make direct comparisons.

The basis of the story line remained, with Kristofferson playing rock star John Norman Howard and Barbra taking over as Esther Hoffman. The new picture retains the decline of Howard while Hoffman ascends to stardom, there is an equally agonizing scene in which Esther is utterly humiliated by Howard, but the end is brought up-to-date by Howard driving his sports car ever faster at daybreak, while Hoffman sleeps in their luxurious beach-side home, until the inevitable happens; he crashes and is killed. As Barbra herself so succinctly put it: 'He's [John Howard] alcoholic. He's seen too many audiences, given too much of himself, so when the audiences have gone, nothing remains.'

The critics slaughtered the picture, but there was much to commend it. The pace, excitement and intensity of the co-stars' changing relationship produced the right sort of contemporary images and the luxury foam-bath 'nude' love scenes between Streisand and Kristofferson struck an authentic balance between discretion and frankness, with Barbra's role model of the liberated, initiating, assertive, expressive rock-age female of the 1970s, excitingly convincing. The sexual chemistry generated by Streisand and Kristofferson had such power and conviction in their more intimate scenes together that this is one sure aspect of the picture, unfairly ignored by many critics, which is surely more than a match for the Garland–Mason performance.

These scenes cannot have been easy for either of them, since some time before they had been attracted to one another and had dated for a while before breaking off the relationship. Nor could Peters have been all that delighted to see his new girfriend in such strongly focused love scenes with her old flame. The on-screen relationship between Streisand and Kristofferson was in unmitigated contrast to what they felt for one another at the time and by all accounts the atmosphere between them during much of the shooting was at times tense, to say the least. To Kristofferson's credit as a professional, however, he did say afterwards that anyone would be a fool not to jump at the chance of working with such a talent as Streisand and he was impressed by her professionalism and sheer capacity to make things work. Interviewed later for television he said: 'I found it a real good experience. I thought at the back of my mind it would be something real good or we would end up killing one another.'

The picture also broke new ground with some of the most adventurous and exciting large crowd scenes ever committed to film. The massive outdoor rock concert was staged at a live happening when 70,000 fans converged on Tempe in Arizona, the *A Star Is Born* sequences being injected into the proceedings. This realism was Peters' idea and it worked brilliantly. The late Dennis M. Pallante reported later in *All About Barbra*: 'He [veteran cinematographer Robert Surtees] kept his camera fluid, using helicopter shots. The opening sequence captures the glaring pandemonium of the rock world, as the paparazzi battle with fans and groupies for a glimpse of the coke-induced singer, John Norman Howard. The love scenes are photographed in soft, earthy hues, highlighting the romantic elements of the story.'

The rock concert sequence was among the most difficult to shoot because it would have been easy for too much rehearsal to ruin the freedom and spontaneity necessary to capture the atmosphere of realism essential for the success of the scene.

Typical of the frenetic way in which filming proceeded was the commitment of Bill Graham, a professional promoter of rock concerts, who worked with Peters in putting the whole thing together in just three weeks. It wasn't expected to be easy, trying to reconcile the pent-up emotions of 70,000 genuine rock fans at a genuine rock concert in 100 degrees sunshine with the uncertainties of filming, particularly when delays are sure to occur and where John Norman Howard is required to drive a motorcycle off the stage into the crowd.

To cap it all Warner Brothers, who were to distribute the film, decided that the whole thing was a wonderful opportunity to promote the picture, and decided to invite the press to the location to cover the shooting. A hundred journalists made the trip and had a field day, interviewing Streisand, Peters and others, and being roped in as part of the film as they went about their business, being photographed by the picture's camera crews.

Tempers frayed and writer James Spada, who was actually there among the journalists, has reported the tensions and arguments which developed between Streisand, Peters and Pierson, some of which embarrassingly escaped to the crowd through the loudspeakers. Peters later admitted that the whole scene was a nightmare. But it was also an astonishing and unqualified triumph, providing a depth and realism to the sequence which could never have been achieved by any other means. Even the most bitter of Peters' foes were forced to acknowledge that he had brought off a remarkable *coup*. He and Streisand's concept was brilliant. They turned aside from the easy way of doing things, by using atmospheric background shots and splicing in segments on a sound stage.

Instead Barbra insisted on recording the musical numbers live to create the realism she felt essential for the important musical sequences. Peters explained: 'We all felt we needed something special. We wanted a real festival, an event.' The fans had been asked to get there at 5 a.m., but the place was threequarters full by 4.30 a.m. Some 35,000 tickets were reportedly sold in sixteen hours. Peters said: 'We worked eighteen hours and it was a spectacular sight as the sun came up.' For Barbra it was a monumental barrier to overcome, facing a crowd of 70,000. 'I was scared ... so scared,' she said, but she faced them fair and square and they loved it. 'Why do the picture?' she called to them. 'Judy Garland was great and all that ... but today is the 1970s, a different kind of music, different kind of attitude ... people ... we're going to do the real thing.' The fans roared their approval. Peters had no doubt about Barbra's triumph. He said: 'She went out and faced that audience. She just laid it on the line and sang. There is nobody that sings like her. We created an event and they came to see us make the movie.'

Many years later that respected British musical commentator Benny Green, in talking about Garland's *A Star Is Born* on the BBC, compared it insolently to 'Streisand's calamitous version'. Even given the benefit that he might well have been talking solely about the two films' musical content, the remark cannot be justified. Garland's songs were musically extremely lyrical and the star was probably at her interpretive best; they were soft, haunting and rhythmic. By comparison, the musical score of the Streisand movie was astringent, overtly emotional, unfettered and raw. But then, Barbra's version was set in the bruising world of rock music in the self-seeking 1970s and needed to reflect the harsher musical elements of the times.

'Evergreen', the love theme from the Streisand picture with words by Paul Williams and music by Barbra Streisand, received a deserved Oscar as Best Song, but the picture is also remembered musically for 'I Believe In Love' with music by Kenny Loggins and lyrics by Alan and Marilyn Bergman, 'Lost Inside of You', with words and music by Streisand and Leon Russell, and a haunting finale with words and music by Paul Williams and Kenny Ascher, 'With One More Look at You'/'Watch Closely Now'. For many, both Streisand fans and others with perhaps a more objective opinion, the picture's musical content was considered magnificent, with Barbra delivering some supremely tender moments as well as managing to look and be as exciting as at any time in her career. The superb 'Woman In the Moon' must be one of the most vivid and memorable sequences of Streisand in concert ever filmed.

Yet seldom have the critics been so unanimous in their immediate response to the release of a Streisand movie. Almost without exception they castigated it, and assessments which were to benefit from a longer and therefore more considered judgement were seldom more charitable. In *The Great Movie Stars*, David Shipman assesses: 'Though it remained clear that she'd never hold a candle to Judy Garland, she [Barbra Streisand] wanted to remake it [A Star Is Born], though changing the milieu to rock concerts; epic battles between her and co-star Kris Kristofferson and director Frank Pierson marred the filming; and when it came out cynics dubbed it "A Bore Is Starred" and "A Star Is Still-Born". Seldom in the history of films had manic vanity been so indulged.' And this assessment came from *The History of Movie Musicals* by Thomas G. Aylesworth published eight years after the film's release: 'She [Barbra Streisand] made a mistake in 1976 with her remake of *A Star Is Born*, in which Judy Garland had become the definitive Vicki Lester of all time. It was self-indulgent and a little insulting, and Streisand deserved the blame since she had had complete control over every aspect of the picture. Director Jerry Schatzberg was fired after shooting a part of the film and her boyfriend–producer Jon Peters directed a few scenes before being replaced by Frank Pierson. A big mistake was to switch the story line from the Hollywood movie world to the rock world of the 1970s.'

There is no doubt that Barbra dominated the film. There can be no argument about the battles which took place on the set and the confusion which sometimes existed. It is possible to understand that the four-letter words used in the script, though realistically accurate in the context of the film, could have been offensive. But, even so, much of the criticism was as unfair as it was illogical, centring on the way Streisand and Peters had gone about making the film rather than the finished product. And anyway, as Barbra was to counter later: 'The creative process is a tense one – tensions are high – it's a very difficult, demanding process.' Allowing that some of the cuts gave Streisand more of the camera than might have been necessary or even, at times perhaps, desirable, her overall performance, and that also of Kristofferson, deserved a much more objective appraisal than the cruel verdict filed by many biased reviewers.

For Streisand, *A Star Is Born* was a very personal statement. For Peters too. Sadly, it was too personal for many of the critics. For the first time in ten pictures she had a monopoly of control and was able to regulate scenes and raise performances to her own exacting standards. It was her own and Peters' picture. Once committed to the project she had relished the opportunity to make it in her own image, as always in all she did, striving for perfection; she was at the same time both mesmorized by the challenge yet traumatized by self-doubt and indecision. She had learned to play the guitar and had lost weight from the fulsome middle-aged Fanny Brice in *Funny Lady* to the smooth, provocative Esther Hoffman. She was confident that she had done a good job, despite the personality clashes on set, and West Coast reviews supported her optimism.

So she was distraught by the hammering she later received from the important New York critics and also by a particularly venomous press article written by Frank Pierson under the heading: 'My Battles with Barbra and Jon' published about a month before the movie was due to be released. This not only went into detail about the difficulties and battles that took place during the making of the picture, but indulged in personal matters between Barbra and Jon which, according to Barbra, should have remained confidential among professionals. She claimed later: 'He broke the confidentiality of the relationship between a director and an actor, which is a very intimate, private relationship that has a great deal of honour attached to it. I was deeply hurt.'

Peters was angry, but could see how the coast-to-coast attention being directed to the picture as a result of Pierson's article could give an additional boost at the box-office. In the end picture-goers showed they could make up their own minds. *A Star Is Born* had its public release at Christmas 1976, a week after its Hollywood première. Within four weeks of its being featured across the US, it had brought in $20 million, recouping more than half its investment within just three days. Soon only *The Sound of Music* was to be a more successful movie musical in terms of box-office receipts and Barbra was on her way to making a personal fortune solely from *A Star Is Born*, since through First Artists she also owned a percentage of the soundtrack earnings. With a massive take-up in excess of 5 million, the soundtrack recording easily outsold any previous film score.

The picture received four Oscar nominations for best song, best musical score, best sound and best cinematography and, as mentioned earlier, was successful in the Best Song category. At the Golden Globe ceremony, Barbra was called up three times for the best song, best musical actress and best musical picture trophies, Peters sharing the last distinction. Altogether the picture won five Golden Globe awards. This was followed in 1977 by success in the Favourite Motion-Picture Actress category at the People's Choice Awards. 'Evergreen', the love theme from *A Star Is Born*, became an international best-seller with a top sale of more than 7 million. It topped the American charts after only ten weeks, while the film's LP took only seven weeks to reach the top and stayed there for six weeks.

'Evergreen' came out of Barbra's insistence on learning to play the guitar for the picture. She discovered that her guitar teacher wrote songs. Said Barbra: 'I thought, God, I only sing songs that other people write – I've got to try to do something like that.' Once when she got bored with her lessons she started fooling around with a few chords; and from that not only emerged one of the picture's most successful songs, but a melody which will forever be associated with Streisand. Another exquisite number, 'Lost Inside of You', with words and music by Streisand and Leon Russell, came from a classical piece Barbra had done years before. There was also a string of other awards including two from Billboard (Top Easy-Listening Artist and Soundtrack of the Year) and the American Music Award for Best Film Album.

Because of the punishment of the film by many critics and Pierson's potentially damaging article, Peters persuaded Barbra to promote the film strongly through media interviews, personal appearances and visits to Europe and elsewhere. This not only paid off but gave her enormous international following the chance to acquire a closer and more up-to-date perspective of their favourite star. The picture also had a salutory effect on Kris Kristofferson. His role as the booze-sodden John Norman Howard was such a personal revelation to him when he first saw the picture that, stunned and shocked, he decided to mend his ways and gave up the bottle.

Peters has said that *A Star Is Born* was always intended to be a labour of love, but Barbra admitted that it was a nightmare. But despite all the volatile arguments, the massive media speculation, and the personal abuse, the movie was completed only one day overdue and within the prescribed budget. Post-production was carried out in a special studio which Streisand and Peters had designed as a conversion for her ranch-style home with editing and sound rooms where, reports suggest, Barbra worked long and tirelessly with a team of technicians, cutting, dubbing and refining. She is said to have found the experience creative, stimulating, but draining after the rigours of the picture itself. She said on television later: '*A Star Is Born* – it was two-and-a-half years of my life.' It took twelve weeks to dub the sound only. And about the character she played: 'I wanted Esther, as myself, to want everything. I want it all and, of course, you can't have everything, but you can go down trying.'

She was concerned after the filming, post-production, interviews, appearances and travels related to *A Star Is Born*, not to involve herself again for a while with another picture and, after releasing six pictures in five years, it was not for two more years that she was tempted to return to a film set, and then primarily as an actress. The new film, *The Main Event*, to be released through Warner Brothers in June 1979, brought Barbra and her former co-star Ryan O'Neal together again. *Yentl* was already on Barbra's mind and she had wanted to make a start on what already had become for her a personal crusade rather than just another picture, but after the often agonizing and sapping *A Star Is Born*, she was persuaded by Peters that another comedy, after the four she had already done, but this time with the two of them working together, would be better.

The film has a prize-fighting background with O'Neal, in private life a former Golden Gloves boxer who had been interested in the game for some twenty years, in the role of an unsuccessful prize-fighter and Streisand generally getting in the way as his novice manager. The setting is an ideal background to a traditional battle of the sexes and the result, according to the *Philadelphia Daily News*, 'produced the kind of carefree laughter that hadn't been provoked since Cary Grant's dinosaur collapsed in *Bringing Up Baby*.' Hillary Kramer (Streisand) is originally a successful Beverly Hills businesswoman, organized and orderly, until she discovers that her business manager has embezzled her fortune, leaving her with the dubious asset of a contract on a losing boxer named Eddie 'Kid Natural' Scanlon (O'Neal).

Hillary is determined to make another fortune by turning Eddie, whose ambitions in the fight game have long since faded, into a champ. The fun centres around their relationship and it was quickly evident that the on-screen presence and sexually charged chemistry of Streisand and O'Neal was as compelling as it had been seven years before in their first screwball comedy together, *What's Up Doc?*

Barbra and Jon Peters co-produced the picture through Barbra's Barwood Films and First Artists organizations, and Howard Zieff came in as director. The basis of the picture was a script by Gail Parent and Andrew Smith which had stimulated O'Neal's interest in doing the picture, the boxing theme enabling him to satisfy a long-held ambition. Barbra was more relaxed and less emotionally committed than she had been on *Star*, but still worked with her customary zeal in her quest for perfection. Said Howard Zieff, who seemed to work well with Barbra: 'Barbra doesn't stop. She wants to find the ultimate performance. She's not one of those stars who say they've had enough – that's what I like about her; she's willing to try it six or seven times. She'll work as hard as you want.' Ryan confirmed the point, adding that she worked fifteen and sixteen hours a day to make sure that everything was going well, but doing it in a feminine way. 'I would never have done the picture without her,' he said.

Streisand and O'Neal both had to get in shape for the picture, Barbra working out at Gilda's Gym, the luxurious penthouse exercise studio. The location was used for a sequence in the film, as were a number of other locations in and around Los Angeles including the famous Olympic Auditorium, a downtown hot-dog stand, and a Malibu beach-side house while the picturesque Cedar Lake in the Big Bear mountains north of Los Angeles became the Kid's winter training camp for a week.

The story line develops as Hillary manages to convince the Kid that they will both benefit financially if he makes a serious effort to get back into the boxing game, and his comeback has got to the point where he is about to win a significant fight when Hillary, who has fallen in love with him in the process, realizes she will lose him if he wins. She throws in the towel and the picture ends with them in each other's arms. Off-camera, the erstwhile lovers might well have retained some remnants of affection for each other, for according to James Spada in

Streisand: The Woman and the Legend, Jon Peters walked into a rehearsal one day to find them kissing, so he just kept on going. But Ryan denied publicly more than once that his affection for Barbra was any longer romantic.

The picture had mixed reviews and even Lynne Pounder, editor of *All About Barbra*, a dedicated Streisand magazine, assessed that it didn't match *What's Up Doc?* though the two pictures, both screwball comedies, were differently focused in many aspects. Said Lynne: 'The earlier picture was a zany comedy whereas *The Main Event* was modern and more sophisticated.' And in the same publication at a different time Allison J. Waldman commented: 'Unfortunately, somewhere between the writing and the filming the guts, grit and giggles were lost in the translation.' The Hillary characterization also comes in for comment. Reports Waldman: 'In one instance Hillary is bright and articulate, understanding the ins and outs of business and the ways to get things done in the world. Two minutes later she's foolishly yelling instructions to the Kid while reading from a "how to box" book. She's smart enough to avoid sleeping with the Kid before she's established a successful working relationship, but too dumb to resist changing the terms of the fight to winner-take-all.' She makes the point that Hillary is so schizo that she's not funny, she's silly, so '... how are we to believe in this character?'

However, *The Main Event* had some funny moments and for the most part was good entertainment, even allowing for the all-too-predictable ending. A particularly treasured moment was the singing by Barbra over the end credits of the specially written song 'The Main Event/Fight' by Paul Jabara, a recent Oscar winner for the Donna Summer disco tune 'Let's Dance', and Bruce Roberts. As Waldman noted: 'Barbra crooned the song's sensuous opening, then belted the percussive disco tune with gusto and characteristic Streisand power.' While accepting its shortcomings against, for instance, *The Way We Were*, Waldman is left wondering, along with many others one imagines, why the song was not even nominated that year for an Oscar.

Out of the nine Streisand films released in the 1970s there is little doubt that *A Star Is Born* was the most eventful. Its making created a sensation. Its release sparked enormous debate and while it failed to win Barbra many new friends among the critics, the public responded with impressive enthusiasm to make it for many people one of her greatest triumphs.

Two important conclusions can now be added, some fifteen years after, to the excitement, turmoil, comment and conjecture which attended its release. On a personal level it gave Barbra her first, if unofficial, taste of movie directing, while in a wider context the picture has gained in reputation and standing over the years. Barbra was personally involved in *A Star Is Born* and showed her enormous promise as a movie maker through her musical concepts, selective camera dynamics, the overall quality of the editing and, as Allison J. Waldman has also pointed out, 'the reflective elements of her own success shown in the screenplay through Esther's quick ascent.' In so many ways the picture mirrors the experience of Barbra herself in what happens to Esther and in the latter's response to a whole range of experiences, including difficulties with the paparazzi, strong convictions, emotional doubts, and her reaction to John's death. It took her back to the death of her own father and she was to admit that it was a very personal thing she wanted to express. *A Star Is Born* not only gave Streisand the chance to extend her creative horizons, but provided the basis for a learning process which would flourish with the making of *Yentl* and decide the course of her own ambitions. For some time later, when asked the question, she put movie making ahead of both singing and acting if she had to make a choice.

As to the film itself, it is now seen more in context and with greater objectivity. The comparison with the earlier Judy Garland version is not so important or valid. The prejudice against Barbra, a female daring to control a movie as well as star in it, and contemptuously allowing her boyfriend with no experience of picture making to help her call the shots, is not so scandalous any more, fifteen years after the event. In the 1990s, Barbra Streisand's *A Star Is Born* can be judged dispassionately and surely stands out proudly as a movie of both excitement and sensitivity, with impressive acting performances and an exceptional musical content. What the public knew from the start, the film industry has come to realize. That perhaps the 1976 version of *A Star Is Born* wasn't such a bad picture after all.

10   *Papa Can You Hear Me?*

Barbara's complex personality which has made her almost reclusive at times, certainly distant in a sense even from her fans, has given Europe too few opportunities to see the superstar at first hand. Her antipathy towards giving live performances means that her enormous following in the UK sadly has never been able to see her at a major live concert, and her media interviews on this side of the Atlantic – even her visits to Britain for whatever reason – have been disappointingly few. Yet on those scarce occasions when she has ventured outside the US she has never failed to make a major impact, no matter how hard she may have tried to keep out of the spotlight.

The first and only time Streisand has performed in public in Britain was right at the beginning of her career when she came to London with the stage version of *Funny Girl* following its smash hit in America. But as the *Daily Express* pointed out at the time: 'American singer Barbra Streisand did more than stop the show last night – she held up the London traffic.' The curtain went up thirty minutes late at the Prince of Wales theatre on Wednesday, 13 April 1966, while first-nighters were still pushing their way through the crowds which had gathered outside. Extra police had to be drafted into the area for what was reportedly probably the biggest turnout of show-business celebrities in recent years.

Among the stars determined to see the latest Broadway sensation were Lesley Caron, escorted by Warren Beatty, Ursula Andress, Italian screen star Elsa Martinelli, Rex Harrison and his wife Rachel Roberts, film producer John Huston, Barbara Kelly and Bernard Braden, and Norman Wisdom, Max Bygraves,

Wendy Craig, Frankie Vaughan, Stanley Baker and the international star Peter Sellers, with his wife, Britt Ekland. Barbra's husband, Elliott Gould, stood nervously at the back of the stalls, and also present for the historic opening of the show, which earlier had taken Broadway by storm, were New York impresario David Merrick, who initially had been associated with the early production stages of *Funny Girl* on Broadway before leaving because of a disagreement with Ray Stark, and veteran British showman Tom Arnold.

The first-night party was held at London's then famous Four Hundred Club in Leicester Square, which had become one of the most celebrated night spots in the world following its opening as far back as 1935. Producers of London's *Funny Girl* had taken over the entire club for the night for one of the most lavish parties in its thirty-one year history. Extra staff were drafted in to prevent possible gatecrashers.

Barbra was in London for fourteen weeks doing *Funny Girl*, but she kept as much as possible out of the public eye. Only occasionally did she venture out, but when she did she made a devastating impact, both visually and because of her comments. In a prickly start to an interview she gave David Jacobs on BBC radio she took him to task at the very start over the pronunciation of her surname. 'Welcome to London, Barbra Streisand', started David innocently enough. She responded almost before he'd finished the phrase with a quiet 'No,' followed by a nervous sort of giggle. Said Jacobs: 'No ... why do you say no?' Barbra's response was: 'It's not Streisand' (her inflection donating a tailing off of the second syllable). 'Now you tell me,' responded Jacobs, perhaps just slightly taken aback by these opening exchanges. Streisand explained: 'It's Streisand – they get equal billing, the Strei and the Sand ... Streisand.' Jacobs suggestion: 'You can put it on two lines?' brought the vexed, more urgent and snappy response: 'Not StreiSAND ... not STREIsand ... Streisand.' Unruffled, the urbane Jacobs scored with ... 'Hm ... but Barbra' – then Barbra, laughing, 'Barbra, yeah.'

But David quickly ran into the brand of Streisand candour for which she was already famous: 'Has this been for some time a burning ambition?' he innocently probed. 'What?' she countered. 'To appear in London ... on the stage,' explained Jacobs. Said Streisand with an honesty surprising in show business:

'Well, that's a little dramatic, burning ambition ... No ... I mean I really want to, you know, but it's not my burning ambition.'

Three days after she arrived in London she upheld her reputation for being one of the kookiest dressers in the business when photographed in a London park in a donkey-brown suit with a double-breasted jacket and culotte skirt, pale-blue gloves and high-laced boots and a tall hair-piece more suitable for a glittering evening out on the town than the stark reality of a March day in Britain. Yet she told journalist Anne Batt: 'My clothes aren't nearly as kookie as they used to be.' Just a month before, Barbra's entirely individual approach to fashion made her one of the world's twelve best-dressed women in one poll, while in another she was voted one of the world's twelve worst-dressed women.

Not in doubt, however, was her reputation as the highest-paid female singer the world had ever known, but she made it clear that more than anything she now wanted to have a baby. She said: 'I'm not a Funny Girl – I'm a serious girl. I never sing in my bath or around the house. I mean, just look at me. I don't belong here, don't belong anywhere. I'm in this singing business up to my eyes and as soon as I've finished the *Funny Girl* movie I want to have a family. It's the only thing that's going to give me roots.' Less than a month later the news broke: Barbra was expecting what was headlined as the 'million-dollar baby' – $1 million being the value of the engagements she would have to cancel because of the baby, due in December.

Only a week before she had signed the lucrative contract for a five-week singing tour of twenty American cities starting in October. Now that tour and other engagements were far less important as Barbra took delight in the confirmation of her pregnancy which she had first suspected, she later revealed, on the opening night of *Funny Girl* in London. Photographers and reporters were waiting for her when she arrived at the stage-door at the Prince of Wales theatre. She looked radiantly happy and after stepping out of her chauffeur-driven car hidden away in a fur coat and dark glasses she shouted that she didn't mind whether it would be a boy or girl. 'I don't care which – just anything will do.'

She later told the press that she and Elliott Gould had been trying for a baby ever since they were married three years before. But good news for Barbra and Elliott was bad news for

London impresario Bernard Delfont, who might well have been hoping to persuade Barbra to extend her contract for *Funny Girl*, which committed her to the show until 16 July. He wouldn't comment publicly about the show's future, but did say that he had a lot of people in mind (presumably to replace Barbra). But when her contract ran out Barbra flew back to New York and *Funny Girl* closed. A nice touch from Barbra was the placing of two full-page newspaper advertisements thanking the people of London for 'many wonderful memories'.

Those memories would have to last a very long time because it wasn't until the early 1980s that Britain saw anything significantly more of Streisand. In the meantime, however, her reputation had soared through her succession of LPs and twelve movies, her latest picture being released in early 1981 through Universal Studios. Her decision to appear in the new movie – *All Night Long* – was something of a surprise because it was well known that Barbra was already heavily committed to *Yentl*, which was widely expected would be her next film to be released. *All Night Long* as a Streisand vehicle was also a curious move on Barbra's part for other reasons, not least because she had earlier turned down the role of Cheryl Gibbons in the movie – the part she had now accepted, and because it simply was not in any way a Streisand vehicle.

Lisa Eichhorn, a young actress who would gain recognition in the 1979 picture *Yanks*, was originally cast in the role, but she left unexpectedly after reputedly receiving a $250,000 pay off. Streisand took over at an extraordinary fee in excess of $4 million, plus a healthy percentage of the profits, for just twenty-four days' filming. Another shock was that Barbra, notwithstanding the obvious financial incentive, had agreed to take on what amounted to a supporting role with second billing to the picture's main star, Gene Hackman. Many critics, conveniently overlooking that such fees were not altogether unusual in the 1980s for top male movie stars, seemed outraged by the size of the fee, presumably for a female performer, and this, together with what they saw to be Barbra's usurping of Eichhorn from the role, might well have coloured their judgement of what was in the end a quite pleasant, enjoyable, romantic comedy deserving more favourable professional treatment than it received from many of the critics.

Twelve years Barbra's senior, Gene Hackman, an Academy

Award winner for *The French Connection* in 1971, plays George Dupler, who is relegated to night manager of a drug store after throwing a chair out of an office window when the drug company fails to promote him. Meanwhile he discovers that his son (Dennis Quaid) is having an affair with a distant cousin (Cheryl) played by Barbra, who is already married. Dupler tells his son it must stop and first meets Cheryl when she calls in to the drug store to explain the situation. He can't resist her advances and they are soon having an affair. When his son finds out he is furious and George leaves home to live in a bed-sit. Under Cheryl's influence George rejects his previous ideas about life and ambition, quits his job and adopts a hippy-type existence. He finally persuades Cheryl to join him and is also reconciled with his son.

All Night Long was not without further speculation and controversy. One theory about Barbra's casting debated at the time was that her agent, Sue Mengers, had manipulated events to bring Barbra into the picture and there was talk of nepotism since Mengers was also married to the director of the film, Jean-Claude Tramont. Press reports followed which suggested that (a) the scenario had been necessary in order to bring a heavyweight name (Streisand) into a picture which was promising to be a monumental disaster; and (b) that Streisand had taken on the role only as a favour to her agent, and was reportedly angry that in such a situation Mengers had apparently insisted on taking her normal ten per cent of Barbra's highly lucrative pay-out, which of course Mengers had negotiated. Tramont, however, insisted that Barbra had wanted to play the part when the chance came up again, in spite of her earlier rejection. Speculation about the whole thing was heightened afterwards when Streisand and her agent parted company.

A three-fold explanation is probably most likely: that (a) she saw it as a welcome diverson from her long and continuing devotion to *Yentl*; (b) after the emotionally and physically draining experience of *A Star Is Born* she anticipated the lesser role of merely acting for such a comparatively short time both refreshing and enjoyable, and relatively relaxing; and (c) the exceptional fee would not have been without its attractions, though too much emphasis should not be placed on this since precedent testified to Barbra's unwillingness to compromise her principles for the sake of an impressive fee.

The picture, nevertheless, offered a different kind of role for both Streisand and Hackman. Barbra, it was later reported, had got interested in the role because it called for a lusty, outspoken and uninhibited characterization – something quite new for her, while Hackman, hitherto known as a character actor, was in *All Night Long* as a featured star. They had known one another during past days in New York and had a healthy respect for one another's abilities. There were no problems on the set and Hackman fully acknowledged his co-star's extraordinary talent. 'When you're working with Streisand you know you are working with somebody,' he said. 'The lady has terrific comic timing. It was a new Streisand, very young, coltish, unprepossessing. Her role wasn't huge, but she did it superbly. She wasn't Streisand; she was Cheryl. And that's acting.'

It was the first time in Barbra's career that she had taken such a non-starring role. She was billed beneath Hackman, but in spite of her being on screen for only about one third of the film, she had a few good scenes and seemed content with what she was doing. This oddball of a Streisand movie, however, was also an oddball in a musical sense. Barbra did certainly sing in the picture, but the song, 'Carelessly Tossed' by Alan Lindgren, was a hideous country-and-western parody calculated to send genuine Streisand fans into a state of near mortification. But the film making continued its unpredictable journey to conclusion as the earlier delays resulting from the cast change which brought Barbra into the project, were now compounded by a serious actors' strike which drifted along for more than two months.

Streisand used some of the delay in filming to travel to Europe with the Bergmans to sort out possible locations for *Yentl* in Czechoslovakia. By the time the strike was over Universal appeared to be as depressed and dispirited with the film as almost everyone else, for they made no real attempt to promote it and the advertising which did support its long-delayed release in March 1981, ran into problems because it was condemned as misleading.

All Night Long was a commercial flop and proved the folly of trying to make a film into something it clearly isn't. Streisand fans felt cheated that Barbra wasn't the star of the picture. Their disappointment soon got around and box-office receipts, which had started promisingly, nose-dived. It had been a popular saying among movie makers in Hollywood that all you needed for a box-office hit was Barbra Streisand. But implicit in that slogan and unfortunately overlooked by the makers of *All Night Long*, was that Barbra was required to be cast in a starring role (and preferably at that time, in a singing, starring role) to make it come true. It was also disappointing for anyone who admires Streisand as an actress and a singer that there had been only one opportunity to see her on film in the intervening years since the release of *A Star Is Born* in 1976, and they had expected something special. They found it an insult, for whatever the reason, now to see their megastar relegated to the role of a supporting player, however convincing her performance.

The picture was a sad experience all round. It was a box-office catastrophy, Hackman was furious over the meagre promotion it received from Universal – it wasn't even premièred, and Barbra was allegedly overheard some time later to say to Lisa Eichhorn when talking about the picture that she, Eichhorn, had been well out of it. But the experience underlined Streisand's conviction to have more artistic control over her movies in the future and gave her new zest to move ahead with *Yentl*. And it was *Yentl* which brought her back to spend more time in the UK.

It had been fifteen years since she had first thought of doing the picture and the idea which had since grown into an obsession, a crusade, finally began shooting at Lee International Studios in London in April 1982. By now there had been twenty different scripts. Earlier thoughts of doing the picture in America had been abandoned and Streisand settled down to a four-week spell in London and three months on location in Czechoslovakia, before returning to London for final production work on the picture.

She had first arrived in London in February 1982, settling into the St John's Wood luxury flat belonging to Jackie Collins at a reputed £1,000-a-week rent. But within a week the news leaked out and a frustrated Streisand, anxious to keep away from prying photographers and requests to give press interviews so she could get on with her work, fled the flat and went into hiding at the Cumberland Hotel in London's West End where she reportedly booked in anonymously as Yentl Auditions. But she was obliged to move on again when this latest hideaway was discovered. She was less seclusive, however, at other times. The national magazine *Woman's Own* later reported that regulars at the Duke's Head, a riverside pub in London's Putney, had stared in disbelief when she made an impromptu visit one lunchtime during a break in filming and downed a pint of best bitter before hastening off the premises accompanied by her minder. And she was spotted leaving a fashionable Mayfair restaurant after dining with actor Michael Caine and his wife.

In Liverpool, she made a host of friends while filming the final scene on the Mersey aboard the ferryboat *Manxman*, on charter from the Isle of Man Steam Packet Company, though she didn't do the media any favours by keeping them at bay.

Streisand astonished even her closest colleagues by her utter dedication to her self-produced movie. Not only was it excessively demanding emotionally, it was physically uncomfortable for long spells since as Anshel she had to wear a specially designed bra to flatten her outline and she wore a wig to hide her curls.

Motivated and inspired by the memory of the father she had never known, Barbra none the less was terrified at the prospect of being a director. She told *Esquire* magazine: 'Everybody is talking to me. I have no moment alone ... I'm getting paid back for all the times I thought I knew the answers.' The feelings were understandable. For a start, she had pursued *Yentl* against almost every scrap of advice and near overwhelming odds. Many had expected her to fall flat on her face when she had taken over much of the control of *A Star Is Born* – and were perhaps hoping, in the wake of the earlier picture's overwhelming box-office success, for a second chance to bellow 'I told you so.'

The fact that she was so much in overall charge of the movie also opened up all the old, tedious rumours about discontent and argument on the set, but in an unprecedented move more than seventy members of the *Yentl* crew and cast signed an unsolicited letter which was sent round to all the major newspapers declaring their support for Streisand. Sent from the Lee International Film Studios at Wembley, England, the letter began: 'The undersigned are currently working on the film *Yentl* which is directed by and stars Barbra Streisand. Because she is subjected to so much adverse press we thought it might interest you to know that during the last three months of rehearsal and filming, she has completely captivated us all.' The letter went on: 'Though undoubtedly a perfectionist, in her dealings with everyone – producers, camera, sound, electrical crews, props, wardrobe, make-up, hairdressers, stagehands, actors, extras, stand-ins – she has shared jokes, chats and pleasantries each and every day. She appears to have no temperament, her voice is scarcely heard on the set, her smile is seen constantly.' The letter ended on a note which must have been particularly consoling to her, mentioning that it was completely unsolicited and '… is the result of our collective affection.' Sadly it made no impact in cynical Fleet Street, only one newspaper making mention of it, though Barbra was given the letter which she then had framed as a valued memento of their gesture.

One of the problems of the Streisand persona is that the media continue to cast her narrowly as an actress or a singer when she sees herself more broadly, also as a director or producer. She rejects the accusation of egotism. 'It is just that I see the total vision of a piece,' she has explained. And in bringing that vision to reality she finds it necessary to be in control of or have a significant influence on many facets of film making. Anything less she sees as short-changing the responsibilities she has to the vision.

That said, Streisand fully acknowledged the essential contributions of Larry De Waay (as executive producer), Rusty Lemorande (as co-producer) and others, including the sensitive front-of-camera performances from Mandy Patinkin, Amy Irving and Nehemiah Persoff (as Papa) to the success of this exceptional United Artists/Barwood film. Her effective working relationship with Terry Rawlings, whose superb editing is another outstanding quality of the picture, is amply evident in the use of montage in the 'No Wonder' sequence. As Allison J. Waldman pointed out: 'Watch the scene without sound and the story is still evident. With the song as vocal commentary, though, the ramifications of all the interplay is dramatically heightened by the shot selection.'

Yentl was a particular vision for Streisand, a personal 'mission statement' if you like, and despite the allegations of her over-blowing and over-dramatizing what was essentially a simple story, it is unlikely that anyone other than Streisand with her personal, innermost commitment could have brought the film to life with so much sensitivity, gifted humour, intensity, understanding and pathos. Even as early as 1979 Barbra wrote a forty-two-page outline of *Yentl* as a voice-over musical with indications where the songs should go and she never lost sight of the idea – assessing, suggesting, rewriting and revising the approach.

Against those who complained that in *Yentl* she did just about everything except pay for the audiences to go and see it, it is as well to remember that not until Mike Medavoy of Orion Pictures suggested that she had a go at writing the script herself, following her disappointment with a number of earlier treatments, did she seriously consider doing so. Amy Irving has spoken of what was probably the most difficult scene because of its natural sensitivity – where Hadass (Amy) has fallen in love with the effectively disguised Barbra (as Yentl) and they are required to kiss. 'She was more nervous than I was,' said Irving, about a potentially awkward, extremely self-conscious scene. They didn't kiss during rehearsals. It wasn't a passionate kiss and Amy said that afterwards Barbra said it hadn't been too bad – just like kissing an arm. 'But she cut it off a lot quicker than I would have,' said Amy. Author Karen Swenson later reported how pleased Streisand was at Irving's handling of the scene. 'I had asked [Amy] to be very maidenly before that scene and she did it beautifully. But then in the bedroom, when she comes on erotically, I asked her to let all her sexiness out, and wow!, did she let it out.'

British screenwriter Jack Rosenthal has also mentioned the commitment required of anyone who works with Barbra. Jack, whose distinguished record as a playwright and screenwriter includes scores of original TV plays and films, stage plays and play adaptations, comedy series and feature films, as well as his writing of some 200 episodes of the internationally famous British soap, *Coronation Street*, said he has never worked harder than on the eight-month *Yentl* assignment with Barbra. 'I think somebody in Hollywood mentioned my name and the first I knew was when the executive producer telephoned me to see if I would be interested,' recalled Jack in 1991. As Isaac Bashevis Singer's short story was already a favourite of his, he was excited by the idea of working on it. Jack explained that Barbra then called and they talked it over at length, and subsequently several times, on the telephone. 'She invited me over to America and we discussed it even more in the small summer house at her Malibu beach home and at her Bel Air house in Los Angeles.'

Jack said he produced the bulk of the writing at his

north-London home when Barbra came over to England and it was a punishing schedule. 'I would spend much of the day talking with Barbra at her London hotel, then go back to my home for heavy sessions of writing until well into the night, before returning to her hotel room next morning to review what I had done overnight and talk about the next stage,' said Jack.

Yentl is a warm-hearted story about a Jewish girl living in Eastern Europe early this century, who is denied the opportunity for a serious study of the Torah and the Talmud, and a more significant place in the world, because of the then orthodox Judaism in Eastern Europe, where in those days the status of women was probably at its lowest. The sentiments are well embodied in the promotional 'standfirst' to the picture – 'In a time when the world of study belonged only to men, there lived a girl who dared to ask ... "Why"?' Her father none the less defies convention and teaches her secretly until his death, when his daughter crops her hair, dons glasses and a man's suit, and poses as a boy to enter the Yeshiva.

Barbra plays the title role of *Yentl* (Anshel is her assumed name to fit her 'sex change') and after joining a group of students on their way to Yeshiva in Bechev, the Rabbi (David de Keyser) is so impressed with Yentl's knowledge that Anshel is admitted as a student. Friend and study partner Avigdor (Mandy Patinkin) takes Yentl with him to dinner at the home of his beautiful bride-to-be, Hadass (Amy Irving) and when Hadass's father breaks off the engagement to Avigdor once it is discovered that Avigdor's brother had committed the unpardonable sin of suicide, Yentl is immediately seen as a prospective bridegroom. This impossible situation is further complicated when Hadass becomes genuinely attracted to Yentl and is only resolved when Yentl, after going through a form of marriage to Hadass but stopping short of consummation, reveals that Anshel is really a girl. In the meantime, Yentl has become attracted to Avigdor, but it is too late. While Avigdor and Hadass are left to marry, Yentl continues her journey and sails away to a New World where she hears that things are different and where, to quote Barbra's own words, 'Yentl would have the freedom to explore her full potential as a human being.'

Location scenes in Czechoslovakia, where some sixty miles from Prague Streisand created the village of Yanev from the farm and three houses which were known as Rozytly, added vivid realism to the impressive outdoor vistas, many of the remnants of the once flourishing Czech Jewish community working as extras on the picture. British-born cinematographer David Watkin was responsible for the magnificent visual impact of the film. An Academy Award winner for his work on *Out of Africa*, Watkin responded to the opportunities and challenge presented by *Yentl* with beautifully composed images which, as Dennis M. Pallante put it, 'extended from the leisurely paced opening shots of a mid-European Jewish village to the sweeping closing shot of a ship filled with immigrants on its way to America, and included the panoramic majesty of the Prince Charles Bridge, the camera's fluid sweep into the village syna- gogue, the elaborate criss-crossing during Yentl's song of elation at being accepted into the Yeshiva, and the atmosphere and feeling during the wedding ceremony.'

Nine haunting original songs from Michel Legrand, with lyrics by Alan and Marilyn Bergman, added a depth of meaning and poignancy to the simple tale which Streisand told with a real sense of skill and understanding. But it wasn't every critic's cup of tea. Some, while welcoming Barbra's return to a singing as well as an acting role on screen, felt the songs neither advanced nor amplified the action, though some reaction was contemptuously irksome and flippant, such as the comment that the music was inclined to burst forth irregularly, 'sometimes from Yentl's mouth and at other times from her private thoughts, and that was confusing.'

The counter point is amply made by Alan Bergman: 'The musical device we discovered for *Yentl* differs from other musicals in that the action never stops to make way for the songs. Instead the music is woven into the fabric. The lyrics are essential to the story, they are seamless.'

There had been no music envisaged in the original concept, but Barbra was extremely happy with the result which enabled *Yentl* to be billed as 'a film with music'. She explained: 'Once Yentl leaves her village she lives a secret life that cannot be shared with anyone. Michel, the Bergmans and I all believed the best way to capture that inner voice was with a musical narrative.' She said she hoped that the music would provide a poetic quality to the film, heightening the emotion of the story as only music can do, adding: 'We worried at first how audiences would react to this device, but there was really no better way to reveal Yentl's unique perspective.'

There was also much talk about introducing the musical element through other characters. Mandy Patinkin, for instance, who played Che Guevara in *Evita* on Broadway, has a fine voice, but it was agreed unanimously not to violate the film's musical narrative as experienced by the central character. 'Patinkin and Amy Irving are free to express themselves – it's only Yentl who can't share her true feelings,' explained Marilyn Bergman.

After the shooting came the post-production and the intricate, painstaking business of cutting and editing the film. Even after her dedication to the concept of the picture, then working on the writing with Jack Rosenthal, directing, producing and her deep involvement with all aspects of picture making including the musical score, Barbra somehow was able to draw on reserves of energy and commitment to promote *Yentl* strongly, both in the United States and in Europe. The picture, which Barbra had movingly dedicated 'To my father – and to all our fathers' was triumphantly received in trade circles and warmly appreciated by people whose opinions Barbra might well have valued.

Steven Spielberg considered it to be one of the most dynamic directorial débuts since Orson Welles with *Citizen Kane*, while Jon Peters, who had been strongly against Streisand doing *Yentl* but supported and helped her once he could see her absolute resolve to do the picture, said: 'I cried when I saw the movie. I sobbed, actually. I wished I had produced it.' In the UK, *Film Review* commented: 'It was such a burning ambition that to make sure she got exactly what she wanted she decided to direct the film as well as take the leading role. She also decided to produce and helped with the writing of the script.' The magazine concluded: 'It is an unparalleled accomplishment fashioned with love and dedication. One can only marvel at the way she has triumphed with the colossal task she set herself.' The picture certainly touched many hearts, not least because of the truly magnificent score by Legrand. Every song fitted perfectly into the fabric of the story with 'Where Is It Written', 'Papa Can You Hear Me', 'This Is One of Those Moments', 'The Way He Makes Me Feel' and 'A Piece of Sky' making a lasting impression.

Within six months of the film's release 3½ million LPs of the soundtrack had been sold, making it the third best-selling Streisand LP behind *Guilty* and *A Star Is Born*. But the songs were never commercially successful as singles, perhaps emphasizing their kinship with the story and the success of the picture as a single story-music concept.

Barbra appeared to welcome and enjoy her stay in England during the filming and promotion of *Yentl*. She was less troubled by the press than she was used to being at home and her days were long and hard. She would rise at six and not finish on the set until six or seven in the evening. Her customary eight hours' sleep was slashed to little more than half that, as she studied, revised and planned well into the night. She kept fit with a few morning exercises, but her short stay at Champneys Health Resort in Hertfordshire, as reported earlier, was cut short when news of her visit there with Jon Peters leaked out.

The Royal European Première in London on 29 March 1984 was a glittering occasion. Crowds gathered around the entrance to the Leicester Square Theatre for the sell-out occasion which was in aid of the charity MIND. Barbra arrived in a flowing long silk, white dress, a long white coat and a matching white turban, and swept into the foyer, pausing *en route* to wave to the enthusiastic crowd waiting on the pavement. Remembering the occasion some years later, Lynne Pounder, a devoted Streisand fan and editor of *All About Barbra* magazine, said: 'We found our seats in the circle and noticed the Bergmans seated down front and Barbra's brother Sheldon seated just to our left. The State trumpeters heralded the arrival of HRH Princess Alexandra and everyone stood for the National Anthem. Then the house lights dimmed, the curtains rolled back and rich bright colours flooded the screen, lighting up the theatre – *Yentl* had started, at last.'

Lynne recalled the scene once the movie was over. 'Everyone jumped to their feet in wild applause ... the applause grew louder coupled with stamping which sounded like a thunderstorm had erupted inside the theatre. Downstairs people had left their seats. Now they stood in front of the screen, facing the circle, their arms raised in applause to Barbra in a moving display of affection and approval of *Yentl* and Barbra's efforts.' The audience began to chant 'Barbra, Barbra', wanting her to stand, but she refused for quite some time, sticking to royal protocol and not getting to her feet until Princes Alexandra insisted. Then Barbra got up and thanked everyone, explaining that this had been the warmest reception she had received for the movie. 'Thank you for understanding the message I'm trying to put across,' she said. 'I made most of the movie here because I love England and I love the English people' and then, turning to Princess Alexandra, she said: 'Thank you your Royal Highness.' Next day Barbra said: 'I was told I couldn't rise before the Princess, so I stuck to my seat. But she was so gracious. She smiled, leaned towards me and said: "Don't worry about me, it's you they want".'

The European promotion included visits to France, Germany, Italy, Holland, as well as London, and she went to Israel also in a frighteningly hectic schedule which included press conferences, television and radio appearances, premières and award ceremonies.   She said at the time: 'My father was a teacher and a scholar and so was Yentl's father. And so *Yentl* was a way of saying I'm proud of him.'

On another occasion she squared a misconception widely held about the basic message of the film. It wasn't about Yentl wanting to become a rabbi – she didn't; she wanted an education, to have an equal opportunity with boys. 'It's about the pursuing of a dream, a girl fighting against odds, about the male and female in all of us which has always been fascinating to me,' she said.

While in Israel Barbra not only attended a première for the film, but was present at an emotional ceremony to dedicate a building to the memory of her father, The Emanuel Streisand School of Jewish Studies. Said Barbra: 'For me this is the realization of a dream and fulfilment of my father's spiritual will. He would certainly have been pleased with the manner of perpetuating his memory.'

11 *More Than Just an Actress*

Over the years the film projects in which Barbra Streisand has been rumoured to be interested have almost outnumbered the pictures in which she has actually appeared. Among those which never came to anything are *They're Playing Our Song* with Elliott Gould, *The Margaret Bourke-White Story* and a remake of the film version of *Gypsy*, while she was said to be so enthusiastic about *Sophie's Choice* (which eventually went to Meryl Streep), that she was willing to do the movie without a salary, just percentage points related to profit.

By August 1985 the latest hot gossip was Barbra's well-known publicized enthusiasm for film director Mark Rydell's project, *Nuts*. This highly charged courtroom drama starring Anne Twomey had run for fewer than 100 performances on Broadway in 1980, but had done much better in Los Angeles, leading to the announcement in early 1982 that Universal would go ahead with the project they had bought two years earlier and make *Nuts* into a picture. It was an idea which had interested Streisand as early as 1981, when she was completing *Yentl*, but the story goes that Rydell wasn't prepared to wait until Barbra was available, though it was unclear at this stage whether she saw herself as actress, director or both. Universal were looking to slot it into their schedule as a fairly low-budget picture, perhaps inhibited in their estimate of its commercial potential by the narrow focus and raw, controversial structure. Not until the project passed from Universal to Warner Brothers was it given greater studio billing. Streisand was confirmed in the project in mid-1985 with a guaranteed $5 million plus a percentage of the receipts. It was the highest earnings ever for an actress for a single film.

In what was widely accepted as her most challenging and emotionally charged performance, Barbra plays a high-class call-girl (from a 'good family') who has murdered one of her clients, but the essence of the movie is her fight to stand trial for manslaughter (which would establish her sanity). Her mother and stepfather, well-intentioned but misguided, we are led to believe, are included in a strong lobby supporting the authority's case for insanity. Only later, through a superbly handled flash-back, do we learn of her unwilling incestuous bathroom escapades as a small girl with her stepfather, a plausible psychological motivation perhaps for her becoming a prostitute in the first place.

As Claudia Faith Draper, Streisand gives what is arguably the dramatic performance of her career and it is not difficult to see what attracted her to the role. The essential truths of the story fall well in line with many of Barbra's personal attitudes to society and life, her intolerance of bigotry and the more stupid elements of officialdom, for example; and the need to be honest with one's self. Not to mention having the guts and strength to fight for what you believe in. She said at the time of the picture's release in 1987: 'I responded very strongly to Claudia. I have always believed in the power of the truth, and how it can get you into trouble. As George Bernard Shaw says in *St Joan*, "he who tells the truth shall surely be caught". Claudia is honest, sometimes shockingly honest; but the truth is all she has and she refuses to give it up.'

Before shooting began Streisand visited a number of mental institutions and courtrooms in New York and Los Angeles. She said afterwards: 'While there are certainly competent people in charge, you also see a number of lawyers, judges and psychiatrists who seem more irrational than the patients. The patients sometimes speak the truth without hesitation and the truth is not always pretty. The truth is not always polite. I found the lack of social etiquette, the directness, the honesty, absolutely engaging and refreshing. That's what I love about Claudia. Without fear of the consequences, she tells it like it is!'

That, she certainly does, with nail-biting consequences for those watching the film, particularly in the early part where lawyer Aaron Levinsky has been appointed by the court to defend Claudia. You fear for her future as she repeatedly cuts into the proceedings, thoughtless of the consequences of court contempt, with savagely delivered instructions for Levinsky as she fights desperately to get at the truth. You feel an almost unsuppressible urge to tell her to quieten down in case she ruins her chances. Immediately you're on her side. Claudia has asked to be spared a life in an asylum and to be tried in a court of law on the charge of manslaughter. Against the odds she wants to fight for that justice and instinctively you want her to win.

Fine performances are delivered by Maureen Stapleton as Claudia's mother, Karl Malden as her stepfather, Eli Wallach as the well-meaning psychiatrist, Robert Webber as the prosecuting attorney and James Whitmore as the judge. Richard Dreyfuss, after first being considered and then moving off to do other things, was finally secured to play the lead opposite Streisand as the court-appointed lawyer defending Claudia. His casting is perfect.

Barbra not only starred in the picture, but also produced it and wrote the background music. After she herself had worked on the original Tom Topor screenplay, she put writers Alvin Sargent and Darryl Ponicsan together for the first time and worked with them to bring out the concept she envisaged. They, along with Topor, were credited for a final screenplay which differed significantly from the original stage script. The effective flash-backs, along with an extended version of the trial which climaxes the picture, also contributed towards a scenario well adapted from the original. Dreyfuss gave an inspired performance, though his commitments elsewhere in the early stages of the project might well have cost him the co-starring role when Dustin Hoffman became interested and was seriously a contender until he named his price and the degree of artistic control he would expect to be given.

One casualty, however, was Mark Rydell. His place as director was taken by veteran Martin Ritt. By this time the project had become so much more ambitious that Warners pitched their budget at $25 million against Universal's original cost estimate of around $10 million. The picture was put out as A Barwood Films/Martin Ritt Production, presented by Warner Brothers.

As with most of Streisand's later projects, there was a message in *Nuts*, there being a strong connection between the picture and liberties and rights, themes of increasing concern to her in more recent years. She said: 'In some cases people can be judged mentally incompetent to stand trial because two psychiatrists say so. Claudia is difficult, and yes, she makes people uncomfortable. But I wonder how many people have been locked up in disputes over manners? In some countries people are consigned to mental institutions because they don't follow the social and political line.' She added: 'People are taking shots at each other on the highways, we're destroying our planet's ozone layer, polluting the water, defacing the globe with a short-term, fast-buck mentality. Now, that's really crazy – that's really nuts!'

The picture also dispels some of the predetermined images of society and shows that one's integrity is not necessarily judged by surface appearances. As Barbra put it: 'Society would look at Claudia's mother and father as wonderful loving parents. He wears a nice tie and she wears pearls on a black dress – on the surface they appear like wonderful parents. And this girl, their daughter, is a prostitute and uses foul language and says things without mincing words. One would judge her to be the bad guy. But you find out through the film that somebody's inner life is maybe quite different from their outer appearance.'

It is likely that with *Nuts* Streisand laid the ghost of the sexual prejudice which had dogged her almost from the beginning of her career. Her central character role is not only intense and demanding in its portrayal, switching through a variety of moods, in turn strident, sympathetic, sullen, crude and savage, but she is on screen for almost the entire film. Add to that her role as producer and score composer, and you might have thought that the new picture would have been the ideal opportunity to rattle all the old skeletons about her being obsessed by her own importance. But this wasn't the case.

In the four years since *Yentl*, Hollywood had probably come to terms with Streisand. For the first time it was able to put prejudice aside and to accept her talent without bigoted reservation. Not that every review was favourable. Nor did it collect even one Oscar nomination; and it was rejected for Golden Globe Awards after being nominated in Best Picture and Best Actress categories. But there were many who still considered it to be an extraordinary movie and more than a few who, like America's Gene Shalit on his *Today* television programme, considered it to be a 'brilliant motion picture'.

Even stripped of its so-called 'messages', *Nuts* was an

excellent film and first-rate entertainment for the average punter. Dreyfuss, who joined Barbra for part of Shalit's televised interview, focused briefly on Hollywood's prejudice against women stepping out of their traditional role. After stating that being definite sets the great female stars apart and makes them compelling, he went on: 'So people might argue with facets of Barbra's personality, or the personality she gives off, but what Barbra is, is definite. And because she's a woman we take issue with that to a greater degree than if she were a man. If she were a producer, star, director of the male gender, we would accept all of her eccentricities in a much more forgiving, normal, unquestioning way. The fact that she is a woman brings all of those things out in very sharp relief, and that's why we're here in a sense, discussing Barbra's personality. We wouldn't be discussing Marty Ritt's personality, or mine, or yours.'

By this time in her movie career, Streisand was well beyond pot-boilers, and after *Yentl* had waited patiently for another film project she could feel passionate about. *Nuts* provided the new challenge and she faced that challenge with her customary devotion, skill and zeal. At one extreme the glamorous, high-class beautifully dressed, sexually intense call-girl, at the other presenting a harrowing picture in prison, accused of killing one of her clients, and in-court fighting with every sinew of her being against seemingly prodigious odds for the right to stand trail as a sane individual.

It was unlike anything she had done before. At the beginning box-office prospects looked exceptionally good. It grossed more than half its outlay within just three weeks of its American release. In London the opening was enthusiastically received and reached number three in the list of top ten films within a week. After that, both in the UK and USA, it fell away, but in the end grossed a healthy $36 million. There is little doubt that, as her father's memory had inspired her to persist with *Yentl*, it was the relationship she had experienced with her own stepfather which drew her to *Nuts*. In fact she said as much to reporters, explaining that Louis Kind had mentally abused her and her mother had allowed it to happen. 'I don't think I had a conversation with this man. I don't think he asked me how I was in the seven years we lived together,' she said. Of both *Yentl* and *Nuts* Barbra admitted: 'I find these films are kind of cathartic. One is given the chance to express certain feelings and they get easier. They get easier to live with.'

Fans of the musical Streisand could take some consolation in *Nuts* from the score which she produced as background music to the picture. It was divided into five instrumental compositions under the title *Claudia's Theme and Variations* and in all lasts thirteen minutes and eleven seconds. Much of it is in reflective mood and gained a considerable reputation when released as an LP by Columbia Records. As reviewer, the late Dennis M. Pallante, observed: 'Jeremy Lubbock arranged and conducted the orchestra and the excerpt, "The Bar" is arranged and played by Randy Waldman. "The Bar" sequence is actually a piece taken from Streisand's *Emotion* album. The original title of the song is "Here We Are At Last" with lyrics by Richard Baskin and music by Streisand. For the film it is used to underscore the bar scene where Claudia meets her john, Mr Green. It is completely rearranged as a cocktail-bar companion piece, sparkled with a jazzy, improvized flavour.'

Other musical sequences are the apartment, the hospital, the finale and the end credits. It appears that Barbra never intended writing any music for the film. When she saw the rushes and heard the music, especially the apartment scene, she was unhappy with the approach. At first she had wanted a score which was not thematic, but changed her mind at the rushes, deciding then that a thematic, romantic approach would be more appropriate as a counter to the stark, powerful nature of much of the film. At this late stage it seems that the original composer wasn't able to produce what she wanted, so she set about the job herself.

Despite the importance of *Nuts* as a major project, on the large screen the 1980s were not very productive for Streisand. She did only three pictures. Musically she was busier and in her private life she continued to make the news. Her relationship with Jon Peters failed to survive the trauma of *Yentl* and by the time *Nuts* was making the rounds on video hire, she was enjoying a close friendship with Richard Baskin.

To receive more media attention, however, was Barbra's later relationship with *Miami Vice* television star Don Johnson, whose turbulent background as a youth was not dissimilar to that of Jon Peters', both fighting the traditions of the system. Johnson is also known for his earlier well-publicized booze binges and for his on–off relationship with the liberated Melanie Griffith, whom he married, and with Patti D'Arbanville, whom he didn't, though their union produced a son.

It was in February 1987, at a party following the Grammy Awards ceremony, that Barbra met Johnson for the first time. Streisand remembers the occasion well enough because earlier in the evening he had mispronounced her surname when, with Whoopi Goldberg, he had appeared to present the Best Album Grammy. Television cameras caught Barbra's reaction as she mouthed 'Strei-sand' not 'Strei-zen'. They met again in December that year in Colorado when they were invited together with many other stars to a holiday party at the ski resort of Aspen. It was a time when Streisand had recently broken from Richard Baskin and, although she and Johnson were seen together in and around Aspen, their first openly public appearance was in Atlantic City when their presence in ringside seats at the Mike Tyson–Larry Holmes heavyweight boxing match in January 1988 caused almost as much excitement as the fight itself.

From then on the media had a field day and the reports were often as doubtful as they were bizarre: Barbra had sent her half-sister, Roslyn Kind, to Canada to check up on Don; Don wanted Barbra to have his child; they were going to be married; Barbra was shopping for an island where she and Don could be alone; Don was being converted to Judaism and Barbra insisted he be circumcized. That Barbra was forty-six, while Don was only thirty-eight, added to the delights of the press.

But their relationship was comparatively short-lived. Certainly nothing like as permanent as many reports from time to time suggested, for as the new decade of the 1990s approached, the romance had ended and Don Johnson had returned to his earlier love, marrying Melanie Griffith for the second time. Barbra it appears is not in principle opposed to marrying again, but to whom and under what circumstances, she doesn't say. Though in many respects a very private person, jealously guarding her independence, she has also said that she likes men and doesn't wish to be alone. 'I like sharing my life with a male counterpart,' she once told British journalist Donald Zec.

At least one of the rumours from that time came true, with one public, permanent reminder of the relationship between Barbra Streisand and Don Johnson. Barbra appeared briefly in an episode of Johnson's television blockbuster series, *Miami*

Vice, and the couple recorded *Till I Loved You* together. The latter, however, didn't make the impact that they had hoped for, certainly not among the DJs in Los Angeles, whom it is said loathed the record so much that in 1988 they collected $4,000 to pay Don not to sing again! It was that year that he met Melanie again and they remarried in June 1989.

That ill-conceived idea aside, Streisand musically by no means let her fans down in the 1980s, releasing nine albums in all and capturing new converts with her exciting pop album, *Guilty*, on which Barbra collaborated with the Bee Gees' Barry Gibb. It was an inspired teaming and elevated their standing in the rock world to such an extent that the record's status remains high a whole decade later. While Barbra concentrated on *Yentl*, CBS took the opportunity to bring out a second grouping of her earlier successes under the title *Love Songs*, being careful to avoid any duplication with the earlier Barbra Streisand's *Greatest Hits, Volume 2*. Remembered particularly for Barbra's superb, and in many critics' views, definitive interpretation of Andrew Lloyd Webber's haunting 'Memory', the album also featured a new version of 'Lost Inside of You'.

The *Yentl* album was released in 1983 and *Emotion* came out the following year. While the former authentically recaptured all the musical magic of the film, the latter struggled in its attempt to register Streisand strongly within a more youthful, contemporary market, mixing rock with ballad. Despite its tepid response, CBS were happy to look at the formula again, but Streisand instead turned to more familiar ground and in collaboration with Peter Marz put out *The Broadway Album*, mentioned earlier. It included eight of Stephen Sondheim's songs and was an outstanding success, gaining the number-one spot in the national charts. *One Voice*, taken from her first full-length concert in fifteen years, was the highlight of 1987 and was followed by the music from *Nuts*, which broke new ground by being the first Streisand album not to feature her singing voice, concentrating instead on her musical score for the film. In 1988 there was *Till I Loved You*, which featured Don Johnson as mentioned earlier, but the album failed both artistically and commercially.

While there was not a lot more which was new Streisand in the 1980s, the decade is notable for the release on video after far too wide a gap of some of her earlier successes – *My Name Is*

Barbra, Color Me Barbra and *A Happening In Central Park*. These combined with video releases of her famous television specials *One Voice, The Making of the Broadway Album* and *Putting It Together* to add a significant new dimension to the Streisand library.

12   *My Name is Barbra ...*

Barbra Streisand was only twenty-one when she first appeared on Broadway and became a star overnight as Fanny Brice in *Funny Girl*. The early 1990s sees her safely into the 'fateful fifties', but despite the intervening years she is much the same sort of person. She is more experienced, more mature of course, and has changed and modified some of her views. As she once told American TV commentator Barbara Walters: 'To change one's mind is good, healthy; it keeps you growing. I want to keep changing, want to keep growing.'

So while her basic convictions about being true to one's self; her honesty; her passion for perfection; being open about what she believes to be right and wrong and working for those beliefs ... while all these remain as strong now as ever they were, her focus on life, what she puts into it and what she wants out of it, have been adjusted by the passing of time. As an unknown she was obsessed by the vision of becoming an actress. Later she was acclaimed as 'an actress who sings.'

In the 1990s, having been a super-achiever both as an actress and an actress who sings, she would rather make a movie than just star in it. It's not surprising. As an actress she always did more than just act. Pushing her ideas and opinions on virtually every aspect of making a movie didn't always go down well on the set and fostered her reputation for being self-opinionated. Yet Barbra says that it has always been instinctive for her to look at the whole of any project in which she has been involved and not just take a narrow or sectional view. 'I visualize things,' she explains. 'I see things completed. I can visualize a film done, a song completed. I see things that I feel need to be done, need to happen.' So the movement from actress, to singing actress, to movie maker – which began with *A Star Is Born* and was accomplished with such distinction with *Yentl*, has been a fairly predictable one for her.

The process continued into the 1990s with the new film, *The Prince of Tides*, which she directs and produces (the latter with Andrew Karsch), and stars alongside Nick Nolte. This romantic drama is based on the bestselling novel of the same name by Pat Conroy, who also wrote the screenplay along with Becky Johnston. There had been rumours for some time that Barbra was interested in the project, but early news put it down as a possible vehicle from United Artists. In the end it became a Columbia Pictures release, with associated billing as 'A Barwood/Longfellow Production'; and for the first time there was the personal acknowledgement – 'A Film By Barbra Streisand'.

Barbra started filming the movie on 18 June 1990 at the small town of Beaufort in South Carolina. Pat Conroy had been a Beaufort High graduate there. The story is about a local shrimping family and covers their anxieties and joys as they face the ups and downs of life. Tom Wingo (Nick Nolte), meets Dr Susan Lowenstein, a New York psychiatrist (played by Barbra) when he visits his twin sister, Savannah Wingo (Melinda Dillon), who is being treated by Lowenstein after an attempted suicide. Although Lowenstein is married to a classical musician – her husband is played by Jeroen Krabbe – she falls in love with Tom Wingo. Well typecast is Barbra's son, Jason Gould, who plays Dr Lowenstein's twenty-one-year-old son, Bernard. Blythe Danner is cast as Tom's wife, Sallie.

Location reports showed that Streisand had lost none of her fixation for authenticity and perfection. Author Pat Conroy was impressed – 'she doesn't even drink a cup of coffee without first considering it very carefully,' he said. 'She puts thought into every single thing she does. I've never met an artist as supremely gifted or as passionate about her work.'

After six weeks of location filming at Beaufort, the action moved to New York where another example of Barbra's meticulous approach to filming was evident. In one scene she and her husband have had a major row and Nolte is photographed storming out of the entrance of a building on to the street, followed a few moments later by Barbra. She cries out to him to stop, he turns back to her and she runs into his arms. To get the realism she wanted Barbra ran up and down the steps in front of the building a number of times so that when they filmed the scene she was breathless, as if she had actually run through the lobby and out of the door.

It was to New York that British screenwriter Jack Rosenthal had been called some three months before filming began. Columbia made the first contact and he spent three weeks in New York working with Streisand in her apartment close to Central Park West. Jack's original brief from Columbia was to 'humanize' the dialogue, but most of his time was, in fact, spent refining the structure of the narrative. He worked with Barbra to a gruelling schedule, similar in pace and intensity to his work on *Yentl*, although this time he did not apply for a screenwriter's credit. After his 6 a.m. hotel alarm call he would work for about three hours before leaving the hotel at 10.25 to be with Barbra in her apartment just down the road at 10.30. They worked together until about 8 p.m. and, after returning to his hotel for a short break and a pizza, Jack continued working until midnight and later, repeating the whole process the following day. The schedule was inevitable since it was essential that Jack spend the equivalent of a full day writing as well as being most of the day with Barbra, going over what he had written and talking further about structure and dialogue.

The shooting of such a major movie caused a stir in the small town of Beaufort. The locals were not used to having an eighty-strong film unit on their doorstep for six weeks, but enjoyed the experience and got excited by all the attention. Many who were successful at auditions became extras as local folk, while some neighbourhood youngsters were chosen to play the Wingo family as children. Three local girls, aged between four and sixteen, were cast as Tom and Sallie Wingo's children. A number of local venues were used in the picture. A makeshift studio at the local gym on the Technical College campus became the interior of the Wingos' house while two other soundstage sets were built at the National Guard Armory some three miles away. Scenes were also shot at the Terry Golden shrimp docks on St Helen's Island, the Bay Street Inn, and the Beaufort Naval Hospital, which doubled as the New York psychiatric facility.

The Prince of Tides is Streisand's fifteenth picture and a $30 million production. Infinite care was taken to make every detail correct. One of the early scenes shows the Wingo twins, Tom and Savannah, having a birthday celebration. One of the local cake shops was called upon to supply the somewhat elaborate double-layer yellow-and-white-icing cake, but in case the cake melted under the intense heat of the studio lighting, five extra cakes were ordered. Another scene called for fragrant, white-petalled, long-stemmed gardenias, the variety particularly favoured by Tom's mother, Lila Wingo, but they had stopped blooming a month before. The problem persisted for a number of weeks, all possible local sources ending in failure. In the end the manager of a local florist was able to arrange orders from hothouses in California and South America.

Conroy's detailed and lengthy volume was not easily reshaped to fit the disciplines of commercial film making and he marvelled at the process. Speaking of Streisand he said: 'Her sheer will is the reason this movie is getting made. She's as smart as hell, to take this novel of biblical length and pretension and break it down into a movie. She's not afraid of anything.'

Since *A Star Is Born* in 1976 Barbra has been more careful in her choice of film subjects. Since becoming more than just an actress who sings, she takes on only those projects which appeal to, and motivate, her. As she once said to Britain's Iain Johnstone: 'When I say I'm doing a movie I put my life into it.' Conroy wouldn't doubt it since he much admired her grasp of all aspects of filming. He said: 'She puts thought into every single thing she does. She will say to me, "Pat, do you remember on page 275 where Tom Wingo said so and so ...." and I would say, "No, Barbra, why?" She would be stunned that I didn't remember.'

Being professionally independent has not only allowed Barbra Streisand to play the roles she wants to play and sing the songs she wants to sing, but has given her time to do other things. At one time her work was everything, but now she is happy to say that it is only one part of her life, if an important part. 'Success is a great thing,' she says, 'but it can't be responsible for my happiness.'

Five or six years ago, as she showed American TV commentator Barbra Walters over some of the forty acres of her Malibu estate with its beautifully landscaped gardens (tended by six gardeners) and five houses, she said how much she loved flowers and space. 'And I love design,' she added.

When she was originally doing the gardens she spent something like three months visiting the local nurseries and got so interested in everything that she was able to use many of the Latin names for the flowers and plants. She had the same compelling attitude when it came to the houses. One house she created in art deco using two basic colour schemes, black to grey and burgundy to pink. She found the decorative arts of the 1920s and 1930s particularly intriguing. 'They were thought out, not random,' she explained and illustrated the point in her own home by pulling a rug away to reveal a rug of tiles beneath. She had designed them herself and had carried the same design through to the light fittings. In another house she featured early American furniture. These were the days of her relationship with Richard Baskin, her nine-year affair with Jon Peters at an end. Staying mostly in the more informal, cosier peach house while living there with Baskin, the other houses were used primarily for guests and for entertaining.

Barbra has definite views about almost everything and has continued to support the causes which interest and concern her. In recent times she has grown more conscious about the natural world and what modern society is doing to it. She has been caught up in the rush for more careful eating and while shooting *Tides* at Beaufort could be seen visiting a trendy restaurant on Bay Street for Diet Center Turkey Sandwich, though she couldn't resist her favourite coffee ice-cream to follow. Focus of Barbra's charitable work is The Streisand Foundation, which supports organizations committed to anti-nuclear activities, the preservation of the environment, civil liberties and human rights. Organizations to benefit through the Foundation range from the National Coalition on Black Voter Participation and the Environment Defense Fund, to the American Civil Union and the Clean Water Fund. She reportedly gave $500,000 of her pay-out from *All Night Long* to cardiac research. Chairs have also been established in a number of universities and the Foundation has established the Streisand Center for Jewish Cultural Arts at Hillel – UCLA.

Barbra neither flaunts nor masks her Jewish origins. She is unerringly honest, explaining her attitude thus: 'It is very important to me to be who I am ... and I'm Jewish.' It says it all and comes from the same kind of basic morality which, once over her first reaction when snubbed by the Motion Picture

Academy over *Yentl*, brought this typical response: 'It doesn't matter to me. The film speaks for itself.' She is in many ways fiercely independent. She concedes without sorrow or regret that the opinion that matters most to her is her own. Yet at the same time she can be refreshingly humble – she would call it being honest – for such an international superstar. 'No matter how big a so-called star you are, you always have to prove yourself,' she says. Repeatedly asked at one time why she didn't have her nose fixed, she would say that she didn't trust the doctors to do it right ... and anyway, 'my nose is sort of part of my face ... it's all a little odd.'

Barbra maintains that most of the stories that have been printed about her being bitchy and bloody-minded were not true. Much of this particular legend leads back to the early days when she became a big star very quickly – 'I was a personality before I was a person' is how she puts it – and she wasn't experienced enough to cope with all the attention. Stories get handed down, are blown up and added to. Some of those things, she maintains, simply didn't happen. On the other hand, she makes no excuse for doing what she feels to be important or necessary, whether making a picture or cutting a record, like suggesting something or speaking out if she feels that an idea won't work or that there is a better way of doing something. 'That is no more than any actress would do who has integrity and opinions,' she says. 'But later I developed more of a sense of humour about it all.'

The public persona is one thing, but to see the occasional television interviews she has been persuaded to give, particularly those in the United States, is to see a different kind of Barbra Streisand. Photographed in the comfort of her Malibu home she has been relaxed, responsive and friendly. The first thing that comes across is that she is much more attractive than you imagine. Her face is naturally expressive and as she talks she frequently uses those long-fingered, elegant hands to make the point. She is extremely articulate with, clearly, a thoughtful and original mind and will think carefully before responding to any question. She isn't one for stock, superficial show-biz answers. She does you the courtesy of searching for words which will let her convey her individual feelings on a subject.

You are struck by her being so 'ordinary'. She isn't performing for the camera, makes no pretentious gestures and is so natural

that it is hard to believe that you are watching and listening to
probably the world's greatest female entertainer of our
generation. Her expressive voice is soft, attractive, well-
modulated and reveals nothing of its enormous range in song
form; nor is there trace of the harsh, babbled, high-speed chat
which is still so well remembered from her crazy early-1970s
movies. She is also refreshingly feminine and you can't fail to be
impressed by her candidness and honesty. When asked her
reasons for not doing many concerts she says frankly: 'I really
don't enjoy personal appearances – they frighten me.' It's hard
to argue with that kind of response.

In fact there is an underlying honesty in any interview she
gives. In her later interviews she is gentler, more sympathetic
and agreeable than in those she gave at the time of her success
in *Funny Girl*, less defensive. Mind you, she'll still correct the
pronunciation of her surname if you get it wrong ... but now
with less vexation. She will still repudiate the 'difficult and
temperamental Streisand' bit – then, with resignation, 'somehow it's become part of my image.' At the same time, she has
said often enough that she was afraid of being misunderstood,
adding: 'People are what they are, I would like people not to be
confused, not to be misled by what they have read.'

It is probably true that your opinion of Barbra Streisand
depends on who you are and the kind of contact, if any, you
have had with her. She is not always the same – she's a 'this'
person at one time, a 'that' person another, accepting extremes
of mood and emotion as the norm and often drawing a slim
division between the two. By her own admission she is simple
and complex, lazy and driven, generous and selfish, unattractive and beautiful. These extremes, once very polarized, have
grown less so over the years, though it is still not surprising that,
when talking once with Iain Johnstone about her sometimes
tempestuous relationship with Jon Peters, she said: 'If you love,
you hate; it's indifference that has nothing to do with love.'

Barbra Streisand is probably unique in that she has remained
an acknowledged superstar in spite of longish spells of
professional inactivity. In the past eleven years she has made
only four pictures, yet her standing as one of the very top
creative actresses and one of the most dynamic personalities in
Hollywood is undiminished. Her record releases are major
events. She could still name her own price for a personal

appearance, while a television interview would guarantee a record rating. It is simply that Barbra Streisand genuinely is, and has been for some time, a legend in her own lifetime. But it's hard to be a legend, she once said. 'You're expected to be superhuman. I'd like to be anonymous ...' at times, but the moral is that you can't have everything.' She hinted some years ago that she might have liked to have had more children and that, looking ten years ahead, she perhaps saw herself digging up the garden, planting vegetables and directing a film. 'I've never been into "enjoying" my life,' she said. 'I've always been working, and working can be a painful experience. I want to make my life joyful and I was never much into nature; I now feel great beauty in nature and enjoy small things like baking a loaf of bread and spending a fun day ... being with my family.'

Barbra Streisand is for many people a magical being. She has prodigious talent, outstanding presence and personal dynamism. As a singer it has been hard to pinpoint the idiom which is hers instinctively. For a long time she made the song fit the voice. Discipline of her own performance before the camera didn't always come easily. But it would take a brave soul to question the truth of Jon Peters when he says: 'Her talent and genius have never been questioned. There is nobody that sings like her.'

Sadly for those who thrill to Barbra's vocal talent, *The Prince of Tides* is by no means a musical. Rumours circulating early 1991 pointed to Oscar-winning John Barry, famous for his scores for *Out of Africa, Somewhere In Time* and *Dances With Wolves,* as well as for the world-famous Bond theme, as being likely to provide the background score for Barbra's latest movie, though later reports pointed to the involvement of James Newton Howard, following his success with *Pretty Woman.* It is hard however not to see Barbra making some contribution to the final outcome. But this new film of Streisand's might still also be a time of celebration for her musical fans. For at about the time of the movie's release, Columbia planned to put out a large collection of rare Streisand recordings, many never before available, covering her entire career. Reported Streisand enthusiast Chris Nickens from Los Angeles: 'From what I understand the package will feature more than three hours of music, including early live nightclub appearances, television work with Judy Garland and Ray Charles, and Barbra's famous acceptance speech as well as her televised conversation with Golda Mier which was part of a special saluting Israel on its thirtieth anniversary. It will be one of the major recordings in Barbra's career.'

An enormous response to both this latest film and the recordings, as so often in the past with new Streisand material, is assured for whatever Barbra does is a major happening in the entertainment business. Her attitude to film making ('It's a very personal thing, to make a film. All we have is what is in our hearts, what is in our soul, what is in our heads') and to singing ('I always sing for myself') is genuinely unique. The need for control, the push for perfection remains. Barbra Streisand is simply ... Barbra Streisand. The words are golden. When you've said that you've said it all for the huge numbers who see her in a class of her own and for whom, in the words of one of her most famous songs from her most underrated movie *A Star Is Born*: 'The world could end each night with one more look at you.'

Filmography

Funny Girl 1968 Columbia
Directed by William Wyler. Appeared with Omar Sharif, Kay Medford, Anne Francis, Walter Pidgeon, Lee Allen and Gerald Mohr. 147 minutes.
 Barbra Streisand gained an Oscar in the Best Actress category (shared with Katherine Hepburn).
Hello Dolly! 1969 Twentieth Century Fox
Directed by Gene Kelly. Appeared with Walter Matthau, Michael Crawford, Marianne McAndrew, E.J. Peaker, Tommy Tune and Louis Armstrong. 148 minutes.
On a Clear Day You Can See Forever 1970 Paramount
Directed by Vincente Minnelli. Appeared with Yves Montand, Bob Newhart, Larry Blyden, Simon Oakland, Jack Nicholson, John Richardson, Pamela Brown, Irene Handl and Roy Kinnear. 130 minutes.
The Owl And The Pussycat 1970 Columbia
Directed by Herbert Ross. Appeared with George Segal, Robert Klein, Allen Garfield and Roz Kelly. 96 minutes.
What's Up Doc? 1972 Warner Bros.
Directed by Peter Bogdanovich. Appeared with Ryan O'Neal, Kenneth Mars, Austin Pendleton, Sorrell Booke, Stefan Gierasch, Mabel Albertson, Michael Murphy, Madeline Kahn, John Hillerman and Randy Quaid. 94 minutes.
Up The Sandbox 1972 First Artists
Directed by Irwin Kershner. Appeared with David Selby, Jane Hoffman, Jacobo Morales, John C. Becher, Paul Benedict and Paul Dooley. 98 minutes.
The Way We Were 1973 Columbia
Directed by Sydney Pollack. Appeared with Robert Redford, Bradford Dillman, Lois Chiles, Patrick O'Neal and Viveca Lindfors. 118 minutes.

For Pete's Sake   1974   Columbia
Directed by Peter Yates. Appeared with Michael Sarrazin, Estelle Parsons, William Redfield and Molly Picon. 90 minutes.
Funny Lady   1975   Columbia
Directed by Herbert Ross. Appeared with James Caan, Omar Sharif, Roddy McDowall, Ben Vereen and Carole Wells. 138 minutes.
A Star is Born   1976   First Artists
Directed by Frank Pierson with collaboration from Barbra Streisand, who was also executive producer. Appeared with Kris Kristofferson, Paul Mazursky and Gary Busey. 140 minutes.
   Barbra Streisand received an Oscar for her composition Evergreen, along with Paul Williams (lyrics) in the Best Song category.
The Main Event   1979   Warner Bros.
Directed by Howard Zieff. Appeared with Ryan O'Neal, Paul Sand, Whitman Mayo and Patti D'Arbanville. 113 minutes.
All Night Long   1981   Universal
Directed by Jean-Claude Tramont. Appeared with Gene Hackman, Diane Ladd and Dennis Quaid. 88 minutes.
Yentl   1983   United Artists
Directed by Barbra Streisand who also produced and co-authored the picture. Appeared with Mandy Patinkin, Amy Irving, Nehemiah Persoff, Steven Hill and Allan Corduner. 133 minutes.
   Michael Legrand (music) and Alan and Marilyn Bergman (lyrics) received an Oscar in the Best Original Score category.
Nuts   1987   Warner Bros.
Directed by Martin Ritt. The film was produced by Barbra Streisand and music was by Barbra Streisand. Appeared with Richard Dreyfuss, Maureen Stapleton, Eli Wallach, Robert Webber, James Whitmore and Karl Malden. 116 minutes.
The Prince of Tides   1991   Columbia
Directed by Barbra Streisand, who also produced the picture. Appeared with Nick Nolte, Melinda Dillon, Blythe Danner, Jason Gould, Jeroen Krabbe and Kate Nelligan.

Acknowledgements

My task would have been considerably harder without the enthusiastic cooperation of a number of friends and colleagues. I would like to thank Christopher Nickens in Los Angeles for his help in the early stages of the project, Maria Seddon, Paul Mungo of *Screen International*, and staff in the stills and library information sections of the British Film Institute and in the various film companies who answered my queries and provided information. My appreciation is extended to Jack Rosenthal for spending time talking to me about his work with Barbra on *Yentl* and *The Prince of Tides*.

My special thanks go to Lynne Pounder, editor of *All About Barbra*, for her considerable help and enthusiasm and for allowing me to quote from issues of her publication. Her unfailing cooperation and interest, not to say her wisdom and knowledge on Streisand matters, was invaluable. I am also indebted to Lynne for providing photographs from her vast collection of Streisand material. My appreciation is also extended to her contributors, Allison J. Waldman, Roald Rynning, Dennis M. Pallante, Steve Whicker, Karen Swenson, Kevin Burns and, specifically in connection with *The Prince of Tides*, Ronnie Durrence, the Savannah News/Morning News and Assoc. Press, and Guy Vespoint.

For permission to reproduce extracts from published material I am grateful to Bison Books Limited (*The Hollywood Musical* by Clive Hirschhorn, and *History of Movie Musicals* by Thomas G. Aylesworth); Virgin-W.H.

Allen (*Robert Redford* by David Downing); Doubleday
(*Streisand: the woman and the legend* by James Spada); John
Farquharson Ltd. (*Streisand* by Rene Jordan); New English
Library (*Barbra, a biography of Barbra Streisand* by Donald
Zec and Anthony Fowles); Angus & Robertson (*The Great
Movie Stars* by David Shipman); Branden Publishing,
Boston (*Barbra, an actress who sings, vol. 1 and 2*, by James
Kimbrell); and Mitchell Beazley (*The Book Of Musicals* by
Arthur Jackson).

Important sources of information, in addition to those
mentioned above, were *The Movie, Film Review, Esquire,
Woman's Own, Barbra Streisand: the woman, the myth, the
music* (Century Hutchinson) by Shaun Considine, *Daily
Express, Long Island Press, Chicago Tribune, Newsweek,
Reader's Digest (Life), Playboy, Salt Lake City Desert News*,
and radio and television interviews by David Jacobs, Iain
Johnstone, Barbara Walters and Gene Shalit.

Index